WORDLY WISE 3000®

3000®
SECOND EDITION

Book **5**

Kenneth Hodkinson | Sandra Adams

EDUCATORS PUBLISHING SERVICE
Cambridge and Toronto

Original cover design: Hugh Price
Interior design: Sarah Cole
Acquisitions/Development: Kate Moltz
Editors: Wendy Drexler, Elissa Gershowitz, Stacey Nichols Kim, Theresa Trinder, Laura Woollett
Editorial Assistant: Becky Ticotsky
Senior Editorial Manager: Sheila Neylon

Printed in U.S.A.

ISBN 978-0-8388-2823-6

7 8 9 10 CRW 12 11 10 09 08

Contents

Lesson 1

Word List
Study the definitions of the words below; then do the exercises for the lesson.

accustom
ə kus´ təm

v. To make familiar.
Every fall the students **accustom** themselves to the new schedule.
accustomed *adj.* 1. Usual.
We sat in our **accustomed** places.
2. Used to.
My eyes soon became **accustomed** to the dark.

alert
ə lurt´

adj. Watchful; wide-awake.
The shortstop was not **alert** and missed the catch.
v. To warn to be ready.
A sign **alerted** drivers to the flooded road ahead.
n. A warning signal.
Because of the forest fires, the nearby towns have a fire **alert**.

assign
ə sīn´

v. 1. To select for a position or for what has to be done.
For this year's basketball team, the coach **assigned** me to play as a forward.
2. To give out, as a piece of work to be done.
Our science teacher usually **assigns** two chapters a week as homework.
assignment *n.* Whatever is given out as work to be done.
What was the **assignment** for tomorrow's history class?

budge
buj

v. To move or shift.
The old metal trunk was so heavy we could not **budge** it.

burly
bur´le

adj. Big and strongly built.
Most football players are quite **burly**.

companion
kəm pan´ yən

n. One who spends time with or does things with another.
My grandmother was always an interesting **companion** when we went to the city for the day.

compatible
kəm pat´ ə bəl

adj. Getting along well together.
Julie and I didn't mind sharing a room because we were so **compatible**.

concept
kän´ sept

n. A general idea or thought about something.
In designing the stage set for the school play, I started with the **concept** of a Japanese tea house.

distract
di strakt´

v. To draw one's thoughts or attention away from the subject at hand.
The police sirens **distracted** me, so I didn't hear what you said.
distraction *n.* Something that draws one's thoughts or attention away.
I do my homework during study period when there are no **distractions**.

jostle
jäs´ əl

v. To push or shove.
I dropped my packages when someone in the crowd **jostled** me.

1

obedient
ō be´ dē ənt

adj. Doing what one is asked or told.
When giving orders, a ship's captain expects the crew to be **obedient**.
obedience *n.* The state or condition of doing what one is told.
We are trying to teach our Labrador retriever **obedience**.

obstacle
äb´ stə kəl

n. Something that prevents one from moving forward.
The **obstacle** holding up traffic was a tree blown over by last night's storm.

patient
pā´ shənt

adj. Willing to wait without complaining.
The audience was very **patient** even though the show started thirty minutes late.
n. A person in a doctor's care.
The **patients** in this part of the hospital are recovering from operations.
patience *n.* A willingness to wait for someone or something without complaining.
Having to stand in line for an hour to buy tickets really tested my **patience**.

pedestrian
pə des´ trē ən

n. A person who is walking; someone traveling on foot.
Pedestrians should use the crosswalk to avoid accidents.

retire
rē tīr´

v. 1. To stop working because one has reached a certain age.
The jewelry company usually gives its workers a small gift when they **retire**.
2. To go to bed.
I was not feeling well, so I **retired** early.
retirement *n.* The state of no longer working.
My Uncle Eli regularly saved money for his **retirement**.

1A Finding Meanings

Choose two phrases to form a sentence that correctly uses a word from Word List 1. Write each sentence in the space provided.

accustom
alert
assign
budge
burly
companion
compatible
concept
distract
jostle
obedient
obstacle
patient
pedestrian
retire

1. (a) become familiar with it.
   (b) do it carefully.
   (c) To accustom oneself to something is to
   (d) To distract oneself by doing something is to

2. (a) is under a doctor's care.
   (b) A patient is a person who
   (c) A companion is one who
   (d) gives hope to others.

3. (a) An assignment is
   (b) A concept is
   (c) a general idea about something.
   (d) something that stands in the way.

4. (a) has traveled a lot.
   (b) A pedestrian is someone who
   (c) spends time with another person.
   (d) A companion is someone who

5. (a) An alert is   (c) work given out to be done.
   (b) a meeting arranged in advance.   (d) An assignment is

6. (a) Patience is   (c) help and support given to another.
   (b) Obedience is   (d) the willingness to wait without complaining.

7. (a) is big and strong.   (c) An alert person is one who
   (b) gets along with others.   (d) A burly person is one who

8. (a) Obedience is   (c) a drawing away of one's attention.
   (b) Retirement is   (d) a time when one no longer works.

9. (a) To jostle someone is   (c) To distract someone is
   (b) to warn the person of danger.   (d) to bump up against that person.

10. (a) go to bed.   (c) To retire is to
    (b) To budge is to   (d) do as one is told.

1B Just the Right Word

Improve each of the following sentences by crossing out the bold phrase and replacing it with a word (or a form of the word) from Word List 1.

1. They expected their children to be **willing to do as they were told**.

2. My grandparents plan to travel to other countries when they **give up working at their jobs**.

3. They refused to **make the slightest move** even though we pleaded with them to step aside.

4. If you and your roommate are not **able to get along**, you should split up.

5. Elido sounded the **signal that warned of danger** when he saw smoke.

6. We made our way around the **objects that were blocking our way** and continued on our journey.

7. A buzzing mosquito can be a **thing that draws your attention away** when you are trying to read.

8. The camp director **gave out jobs and sent** us to the kitchen crew.

9. You see very few **people out walking** this early in the morning.

10. My sister is more **willing to accept delays without complaining** than I am.

1C Applying Meanings

Circle the letter of each correct answer to the questions below. A question may have more than one correct answer.

1. Which of the following could be an **obstacle**?
   - (a) lack of money
   - (b) a fallen tree
   - (c) poor eyesight
   - (d) a pleasant voice

2. In which of the following places would a **pedestrian** be?
   - (a) on the sidewalk
   - (b) inside a car
   - (c) in a favorite armchair
   - (d) on a plane

3. Which of the following could **distract** someone?
   - (a) loud noises
   - (b) whispering
   - (c) dreams
   - (d) the radio

4. Which of the following usually learn **obedience**?
   - (a) dogs
   - (b) soldiers
   - (c) cats
   - (d) children

5. Which of the following must be **alert**?
   - (a) a watchman
   - (b) a babysitter
   - (c) a driver
   - (d) a pilot

6. Which of the following would you expect to be **compatible**?
   - (a) friends
   - (b) partners
   - (c) enemies
   - (d) teammates

7. Which of the following could be **assigned**?
   - (a) jobs
   - (b) rooms
   - (c) seats
   - (d) birthdays

8. Which of the following might make a good **companion**?
   - (a) a dog
   - (b) a canoe
   - (c) a friend
   - (d) a meal

accustom
alert
assign
budge
burly
companion
compatible
concept
distract
jostle
obedient
obstacle
patient
pedestrian
retire

1D Word Study

Synonyms are words that have the same or close to the same meaning. *Vanish* and *disappear* are synonyms. Both words have to do with passing out of sight.

Circle the two words that are synonyms in each group of four below.

1. budge	warn	shift	accustom
2. distract	return	retire	quit
3. concept	barrier	venture	obstacle
4. warning	light	sound	alert
5. jostle	shove	assign	choose

Antonyms are pairs of words whose meanings are opposite or nearly opposite to each other. *Rise* and *fall* are antonyms. Both words have to do with movement, but in different directions.

Circle the two words that are antonyms in each group of four below.

6. alert	drowsy	compatible	patient
7. familiar	slight	alert	burly
8. precious	dreary	unfamiliar	accustomed
9. unsteady	obedient	defiant	watchful
10. assign	retire	jostle	arise

1E Passage

Read the passage below; then complete the exercise that follows.

Friends for Life

The **concept** that trained dogs could act as eyes for those who could not see developed at the beginning of the twentieth century in Germany in an unusual school. The pupils were not humans, but dogs who were taught how to lead people who were blind. The idea caught on quickly, and guide dogs, or Seeing Eye dogs as they are also known, began to be trained in many countries. They are now a familiar sight. These **patient** and loyal animals lead their blind **companions** everywhere they go, permitting them to make their way in the world almost as well as sighted persons.

Not every breed of dog makes a good guide. Seeing Eye dogs must be **alert** at all times, so dogs that are easily **distracted** are not suitable. Labrador retrievers, German shepherds, and boxers make excellent guides because they are smart, easy to train, and usually get along well with people. During its training, the dog is taken to many kinds of busy places. This is to get it **accustomed** to anything that might happen. A dog is trained in large stores, noisy airports, and crowded restaurants. It rides on buses and in taxis. It is pushed and poked, and it learns to ignore anything that might cause its attention to wander.

The Seeing Eye dog is responsible for steering its owner carefully past any **obstacles**. On busy sidewalks, the dog must skillfully weave its way around other **pedestrians** to make sure its owner doesn't get **jostled**. A guide dog is trained to come to a stop just before it reaches a curb; this is the way it tells its owner to take a step up or down. But even though it learns to be **obedient**, a guide dog is also taught that sometimes it must disobey. For example, if its owner tells it to cross a street when a car is coming, it won't **budge** until it is safe to cross. While it is being trained, a guide dog is never punished for making a mistake; instead it is encouraged to do better by being rewarded when it behaves correctly.

When the training is complete, a guide dog is **assigned** to its new owner. The two of them need to be **compatible** because they will be together for a long time. The size, weight, and nature of both are taken into account. A **burly** person might be more comfortable with a large dog while a person who spends most of the day inside probably will not want to be matched with a frisky dog that needs plenty of exercise. From the beginning, a strong bond needs to form between the dog and the owner.

The Seeing Eye headquarters in Morristown, New Jersey, was the first, and is still the largest, school for guide dogs in the United States. Every year several hundred blind people spend a month there learning how to work with the dogs they have been matched with. Usually a guide dog stays with its owner for about ten years before it **retires**. Then, it often may go to live with friends of the owner and stay with them as an ordinary family pet for the rest of its life.

Answer each of the following questions in the form of a sentence. If a question does not contain a vocabulary word from this lesson's word list, use one in your answer. Use each word only once. Questions and answers will then contain all fifteen words (or forms of the words).

1. What was the **concept** behind the Seeing Eye dog movement?

2. When does the relationship between guide dog and owner officially begin?

3. What sort of dog might a **burly** person be matched up with?

4. Why do you think a powerful dog would not be matched with someone who is not very strong?

5. Where are you most likely to see **pedestrians**?

6. **Obedience** is important in dogs kept as pets. Why is this not always true of guide dogs?

7. Why is pushing and poking a guide dog necessary during its training?

8. What is the meaning of **alert** as it is used in the passage?

9. How will a guide dog respond if it is ordered to cross a street with heavy traffic?

10. Why are guide dogs unlikely to get excited when another dog approaches?

11. What is the meaning of **patient** as it is used in the passage?

12. Name three **obstacles** that a guide dog might have to deal with on the street.

13. Why do guide dogs need to keep a watchful eye on other people in crowded places?

14. What is the meaning of **retires** as it is used in the passage?

15. Why would it be somewhat surprising to see a guide dog without its owner?

FUN & FASCINATING FACTS

Alert comes from the Italian *all'erta*, which meant "acting as a lookout on a watchtower." The person in the watchtower had to be *alert* (*adjective*, meaning "watchful"); the person would *alert* the others in the event of danger (*verb*, meaning "to warn") by sounding the *alert* (*noun*, meaning "warning signal"). To be *on the alert* means "to be watchful and ready."

If you live with or travel with a **companion**, you will probably eat your meals together. This was the case with the Romans, too. The word comes from the Latin prefix *com-*, which means "with," and the word *panis*, which is Latin for "bread." To the Romans, a *companion* was a person with whom one shared a meal, of which bread was one of the main items.

A **pedestrian** is a person who gets around on foot. A *pedal* is a lever operated by the foot. A *quadruped* is a creature with four feet, while a *centipede* supposedly has 100 feet (it actually has about seventy). All of these words come from the Latin *ped-*, whose meaning you can probably guess.

Lesson 2

➤ **Word List** Study the definitions of the words below; then do the exercises for the lesson.

aroma
ə rō´ mə

n. A smell or odor, especially a pleasant one.
The **aroma** of hot buttered popcorn made our mouths water.

beverage
bev´ ər ij

n. A liquid used as a drink.
When we ordered our **beverages**, I chose lemonade.

bland
bland

adj. 1. Lacking a strong flavor.
Patients with stomach problems eat **bland** foods like chicken soup and mashed potatoes.
2. Not irritating, exciting, or disturbing.
The doctor's **bland** manner soon calmed the crying child.

brittle
brit´ l

adj. Easily broken; not flexible.
Candy canes are **brittle** and should be handled with care.

cluster
klus´ tər

n. A number of similar things grouped together.
Clusters of brightly colored flowers grew along the side of the road.
v. To gather or come together in a group.
The children **clustered** around the storyteller.

combine
kəm bīn´

v. To join or bring together.
We **combine** oil and vinegar to make the salad dressing.
combination *n.* A joining or bringing together.
Our team's victory resulted from a **combination** of hard work and good luck.

consume
kən sōōm´

v. 1. To use up.
Piano practice **consumes** all of Alex's free time.
2. To eat or drink.
A horse **consumes** fifty pounds of hay a day.
3. To do away with or destroy.
The forest fire **consumed** over two thousand acres in Oregon.

crave
krāv

v. To have a strong desire for.
When he was a teenager, Abraham Lincoln **craved** knowledge so much that he would walk miles to borrow a book he had not read.
craving *n.* A strong desire.
After the hike, we all had a **craving** for lots of cool water.

cultivate
kul´ ti vāt

v. 1. To prepare land for the growing of crops.
Before the spring planting, farmers **cultivate** the soil.
2. To grow or to help to grow.
Ana **cultivates** tomatoes every year in her garden.
3. To encourage development by attention or study.
Parents can **cultivate** a love of nature in their children by taking them on hikes in the country.

equivalent
ē kwiv´ ə lənt

adj. Equal to.
Although the decimal 0.5 and the fraction $\frac{1}{2}$ appear to be different, they are **equivalent** amounts.
n. That which is equal to.
One year of a dog's life is the **equivalent** of seven human years.

export
ek spôrt´

v. To send goods to another country for sale.
Colombia **exports** coffee to countries all over the world.
n. (eks´ port) Something exported.
Grain is an important **export** of the United States.

extract
ek strakt´

v. 1. To remove or take out.
Dr. Bogasian will **extract** my wisdom tooth next week.
2. To obtain with an effort.
I **extracted** a promise from them to leave us alone.
n. (eks´ trackt) Something removed or taken out.
Vanilla **extract** comes from the seedpods of vanilla plants.

introduce
in trə doos´

v. 1. To cause to know; to make known by name.
Let me **introduce** you to my companion, Jane Willow.
2. To bring to the attention of, especially for the first time.
It was our friends in Hawaii who **introduced** us to scuba diving.
3. To bring into use.
The invention of the airplane **introduced** a new way of traveling.
introduction *n.* (in trə duk´shən) 1. Something spoken or written before the main part.
We read the **introduction** before going on to the rest of *The Woman in White*.
2. The act of being made known by name.
After my **introduction** to the others in the room, I relaxed and enjoyed the party.

purchase
pur´ chəs

v. To buy.
My parents **purchase** a new car every five years.
n. 1. Something that is bought.
Store detectives may ask you to show sales slips for your **purchases** as you leave.
2. The act of buying.
Because of a bicycle's cost, I looked at and rode several before I made a **purchase**.

tropical
träp´ i kəl

adj. 1. Of, from, or similar to the regions near the equator.
Ecuador, which lies on the equator, is a **tropical** country.
2. Hot and moist.
The chilly autumn temperature outside made the air at the indoor pool feel **tropical**.

2A Finding Meanings

Choose two phrases to form a sentence that correctly uses a word from Word List 2. Write each sentence in the space provided.

1. (a) An aroma is
   (b) a pleasant smell.

   (c) A cluster is
   (d) a drink.

2. (a) to give it away.
   (b) to use it up.

   (c) To crave something is
   (d) To consume something is

3. (a) An extract is something
   (b) that is bought.

   (c) An equivalent is something
   (d) that is equal to something else.

4. (a) A cluster is
   (b) An export is

   (c) a group of similar things.
   (d) something that is given away.

5. (a) A combination is
   (b) An introduction is

   (c) a strong desire.
   (d) a making known by name.

6. (a) Something that is brittle
   (b) lacks a strong flavor.

   (c) Something that is bland
   (d) bends easily.

aroma
beverage
bland
brittle
cluster
combine
consume
crave
cultivate
equivalent
export
extract
introduce
purchase
tropical

7. (a) is to borrow it from that person.
   (b) is to make that person aware of it.

   (c) To introduce someone to a book
   (d) To purchase a book for someone

8. (a) obtain it with an effort.
   (b) reject it.

   (c) To extract an offer is to
   (d) To crave an offer is to

9. (a) breaks easily.
   (b) Something that is tropical

   (c) has a strong smell.
   (d) Something that is brittle

10. (a) A beverage is
    (b) A purchase is

    (c) something that is eaten.
    (d) something that is bought.

2B Just the Right Word

Improve each of the following sentences by crossing out the bold phrase and replacing it with a word (or a form of the word) from Word List 2.

1. Milk, juice, and other **liquids suitable for drinking** are on sale at the booth.

2. This machine **takes out** the juice from oranges.

3. These computers are being **sold to other countries** at the rate of two hundred a day.

4. Inline skates were **first brought into use** in the U.S. in the 1980s.

5. The **mixing together** of blue and yellow paint produces green.

6. Plants will not grow well if the soil has not been **properly prepared for the growing of crops**.

7. The summer climate in Washington, D.C., is almost **like that near the equator**.

8. After my cousins **paid money in order to own** a dog, they all helped to feed, train, and exercise it.

9. It was clear that Uncle Paul **had a strong desire for** a piece of my mother's pumpkin pie.

10. Every morning chickadees **gather in a group** around our bird feeder.

2C Applying Meanings

Circle the letter of each correct answer to the questions below. A question may have more than one correct answer.

1. Which of the following is a **bland** food?
   (a) oatmeal
   (b) hot chili
   (c) white bread
   (d) pepperoni pizza

2. Which of the following can be **purchased**?
   (a) good health
   (b) diseases
   (c) automobiles
   (d) energy

3. Which of the following can be **cultivated**?
   (a) corn
   (b) water
   (c) an interest in science
   (d) the soil

4. Which of the following has an **aroma**?
   - (a) the number 7
   - (b) freshly ground coffee
   - (c) a famous person's name
   - (d) a rose

5. Which of the following can be **consumed**?
   - (a) vegetables
   - (b) sleep
   - (c) fuel
   - (d) plants

6. Which of the following is a **beverage**?
   - (a) milk
   - (b) water
   - (c) chocolate ice cream
   - (d) hot chocolate

7. Which of the following are **equivalent** to a dollar?
   - (a) fifty cents
   - (b) ten dimes
   - (c) four quarters
   - (d) twenty nickels

8. Which of the following are **exported** from the U.S.?
   - (a) kangaroos
   - (b) grains
   - (c) parrots
   - (d) medicines

2D Word Study

The prefix *pre-* means "before." The <u>pre</u>face of a book is the part that comes <u>before</u> the rest of the book. A <u>pre</u>view of a movie is a showing of it <u>before</u> the general public gets to see it. A <u>pre</u>fix is the part of a word that comes <u>before</u> the rest.

Some prefixes turn a word into its opposite. These prefixes include the following:

un- (an unhappy person is <u>not</u> happy)

in- (an incorrect answer is <u>not</u> correct)

im- (an impossible task is one that is <u>not</u> possible)

dis- (a disagreeable person is one who is <u>not</u> agreeable)

ir- (an irregular verb is one that is <u>not</u> regular)

Change each of the words below into its opposite by adding the correct prefix. Check each of your answers in a dictionary to be sure you have formed a proper word.

aroma

beverage

bland

brittle

cluster

combine

consume

crave

cultivate

equivalent

export

extract

introduce

purchase

tropical

1. mature _____

2. accustomed _____

3. complete _____

4. compatible _____

5. resistible _____

6. obedient _____

7. patient   _____

8. dismayed   _____

9. sufficient   _____

10. like   _____

11. honest   _____

12. easy   _____

2E Passage   Read the passage below; then complete the exercise that follows.

When Money Grew on Trees

Do you wish that chocolate grew on trees? Well, it does. The trees are cocoa trees and they grow in **tropical** countries. Of course, you wouldn't recognize the little pale-colored and bitter-tasting beans of the cocoa tree as chocolate, but they are the raw material from which candy bars are made.

Cocoa trees were first **cultivated** in Central and South America, but are now grown in many other parts of the world, including West Africa, the Caribbean, and southern Asia. They grow best in areas with a year-round temperature of around eighty degrees and an annual rainfall of eighty inches or more. Because the young trees need to be sheltered from direct sunlight, banana plants, which are taller, are often grown between the rows to provide shade.

Pods as big as footballs grow from the branches and trunks of the trees. Inside each pod is a **cluster** of twenty to forty cocoa beans, each inside its own thin shell. Workers cut the pods from the trees by hand and split them open to remove the beans, which are separated and stored in boxes for about a week. When the beans are brown and have a slight chocolate **aroma**, they are ready to be dried, either in the sun or in ovens. After the drying is completed, the beans are put in sacks and **exported** to countries all over the world.

Now they are ready to be made into chocolate. First, the beans are roasted. This makes the shells **brittle** and easy to separate from the beans, which next are ground into a paste. This paste contains a lot of fat, called cocoa butter, which is **extracted**. What remains is cocoa powder, used for making chocolate cakes, cookies, and puddings. The soft, sweet chocolate in candy is made by **combining** the cocoa powder with cocoa butter, sugar, and dried milk.

The Spanish explorers who traveled through Central and South America in the 1500s were the first to **introduce** chocolate into Europe. The Aztecs, who lived in what is now Mexico, ground up cocoa beans and made the paste into a cold **beverage.** They must have thought it tasted **bland** because they mixed it with chili peppers and other spices. Not surprisingly, the name "chocolate" comes from an Aztec word meaning "bitter drink." Montezuma, the Aztec king, seems to have had a **craving** for it because, according to Aztec records, he **consumed** up to fifty cups of chocolate a day!

The Aztecs also used cocoa beans as money. A rabbit cost ten beans, while a slave could be **purchased** for a hundred; that would have made the value of a human being **equivalent** to ten rabbits! This may seem surprising, but here is something else to think about: the Aztecs really did live in a land where money grew on trees.

Answer each of the following questions in the form of a sentence. If a question does not contain a vocabulary word from this lesson's word list, use one in your answer. Use each word only once. Questions and answers will then contain all fifteen words (or forms of the words).

1. How can one satisfy a **craving** for chocolate?

2. What are two ways that cocoa is used today?

3. What is the meaning of **cultivated** as it is used in the passage?

4. Why do cocoa trees grow only in **tropical** countries?

5. To which countries are cocoa beans **exported**?

6. In addition to using cocoa beans for a drink, in what other way did the Aztecs use them?

7. How is chocolate candy made?

8. What would you find if you split open a pod of the cocoa tree?

9. How do workers know when the cocoa beans are ready to be dried?

10. What is the meaning of **consumed** as it is used in the passage?

11. When can the shells of cocoa beans be removed easily from the beans?

12. How is ground cocoa bean paste turned into cocoa powder?

13. How and when did Europeans learn about chocolate?

14. What is the meaning of **bland** as it is used in the passage?

15. Why could an Aztec receive five rabbits in exchange for fifty cocoa beans?

FUN & FASCINATING FACTS

Aroma once meant a spice. Spices have strong and pleasant smells, and in time the meaning of the word changed. An aroma became the pleasant smell of the spice rather than the spice itself. Later the word came to mean any smell, but especially one that is pleasant.

The word **export** is formed from the Latin prefix *ex-*, meaning "out," and the Latin root *port*, meaning "carry." Goods being *exported* are *carried* by boat or plane *out* of the country. The antonym of *export* is *import*. To *import* goods is to bring them *into* a country. (The United States *imports* many cars from Japan.)

The Latin *tractus* means "drawn" or "pulled" and forms the root of several English words. A *tractor* is a vehicle used to pull farm machinery. A *protracted* explanation is one that is drawn out and goes on too long. This root joins with the Latin prefix *ex-*, meaning "out," to form the word **extract.**

The adjective **tropical** is formed from the word *tropic*. The Tropic of Cancer and the Tropic of Capricorn are two imaginary lines going around the earth, north and south of the equator. They are three thousand miles apart, and the area of the world between them is called the tropics. Most of Africa and Central and South America and parts of Asia are in the tropics.

Lesson 3

Word List Study the definitions of the words below; then do the exercises for the lesson.

ancestor
an´ ses tər

n. 1. A person from whom one is descended.
My **ancestors** came from Italy.
2. An early kind of animal from which later ones have developed; a forerunner.
The dog-sized mesohippus is the **ancestor** of the modern horse.

carnivore
kär´ ni vôr

n. A flesh-eating animal.
Carnivores have sharp, pointed teeth that enable them to tear the meat they eat.
carnivorous *adj.* (kär niv´ ər əs) Flesh-eating.
Although dogs are **carnivorous**, they will often eat other foods besides meat.

comprehend
käm prē hend´

v. To understand.
If you don't **comprehend** the question, let me know and I will word it differently.
comprehension *n.* The act of understanding; the ability to understand.
Pawel cannot speak Spanish very well, but his **comprehension** is quite good.

duration
door ā´ shən

n. The time during which something lasts or continues.
We stayed in our house for the **duration** of the heavy downpour.

evident
ev´ ə dənt

adj. Easy to see and understand; obvious, clear.
It is **evident** from your manner that you are not happy to see me.

extinct
ek stiŋkt´

adj. 1. No longer existing or living.
The giant woolly mammoth became **extinct** about ten thousand years ago.
2. No longer active.
Mount Saint Helens was believed to be an **extinct** volcano until it suddenly became active in 1980.

ferocious
fə rō´ shəs

adj. Savage; fierce.
Doberman pinschers make **ferocious** guard dogs.
ferocity *n.* (fə räs´ ə tē) The state or quality of being fierce.
The **ferocity** of the storm surprised us.

gigantic
jī gan´ tik

adj. Very large; like a giant in size.
The *Spruce Goose* was a **gigantic** airplane that made only one flight.

obscure
äb skyoor´

v. To cover up or keep from being seen.
Clouds **obscured** the moon.
adj. 1. Hard to see; hidden.
The boat was an **obscure** shape in the mist.
2. Not easy to understand.
The poem was full of **obscure** words like "clough" and "moraine."

option äp´ shən	*n.* Choice, or something that is available as a choice. We had the **option** of practicing soccer during the lunch break or after school. **optional** *adj.* Left to choice. Bill said we should attend the meeting, but staying for the party afterward was **optional**.
premature prē mə choor´	*adj.* Too early; happening or arriving before the proper time. **Premature** babies require special care before they are allowed to leave the hospital.
preserve prē zurv´	*v.* 1. To save; to keep from harm; to protect. This law will help to **preserve** the old forests in the national parks. 2. To keep from rotting or spoiling. Steve and Martha **preserve** the peaches from their orchard by canning them.
prey prā	*n.* 1. An animal that is hunted for food. Chickens are the natural **prey** of foxes. 2. One that is helpless or unable to resist attack; a victim. Be alert when you travel so that you will not be **prey** to thieves. *v.* 1. To hunt (animals) for food. Wolves **prey** on the weakest deer in the herd. 2. To take from or rob using violence or trickery. The pickpockets **preyed** on newly arrived tourists, who were usually concentrating on their surroundings.
puny pyōō´ nē	*adj.* 1. Weak. Lifting weights can change **puny** muscles into powerful ones. 2. Lacking in size, strength, or power. My one dollar offering seemed **puny** compared to what others gave.
survive sər vīv´	*v.* 1. To stay alive where there is a chance of dying or being killed. Only three passengers **survived** the plane crash. 2. To continue living or existing through a threatening situation. Only two of the eight maple trees in our yard **survived** the hurricane. **survivor** *n.* One who stays alive while others die. **Survivors** of the shipwreck floated on life rafts until the helicopter could pick them up.

3A Finding Meanings

Choose two phrases to form a sentence that correctly uses a word from Word List 3. Write each sentence in the space provided.

1. (a) it is easy to see.
   (b) If something is evident,
   (c) If something is premature,
   (d) it has lasted for a long time.

2. (a) from whom one is descended.
   (b) who does not eat meat.
   (c) An ancestor is someone
   (d) A survivor is someone

3. (a) To prey on wildlife is to   (c) keep it from harm.
   (b) To preserve wildlife is to   (d) have a complete understanding of it.

4. (a) A gigantic volcano is one that   (c) is no longer active.
   (b) An extinct volcano is one that   (d) is hidden from view.

5. (a) is to let it get away.   (c) To prey on something
   (b) To obscure something   (d) is to hunt it for food.

6. (a) The comprehension of something is   (c) the length of time it is delayed.
   (b) the length of time that it lasts.   (d) The duration of something is

7. (a) that is very big.   (c) A puny figure is one
   (b) that is well known.   (d) A gigantic figure is one

8. (a) is one that has not died out.   (c) A practice that is optional
   (b) is one that seems strange.   (d) A practice that survives

9. (a) one that leaves nothing out.   (c) An obscure report is
   (b) A premature report is   (d) one that is hard to understand.

10. (a) A ferocious creature is   (c) An extinct creature is
    (b) one that has died out.   (d) one that eats only meat.

ancestor

carnivore

comprehend

duration

evident

extinct

ferocious

gigantic

obscure

option

premature

preserve

prey

puny

survive

3B Just the Right Word

Improve each of the following sentences by crossing out the bold phrase and replacing it with a word (or a form of the word) from Word List 3.

1. The house was **hidden from view** by a thick hedge.

2. My two-horsepower engine is **lacking in power** compared to the fifty-horsepower one in your boat.

3. It is **easy to see** from the dishes in the sink that someone has already eaten lunch.

4. The film captures the **fierce behavior** of a mother tiger defending her cubs.

5. The pirate Blackbeard **attacked and robbed the people** on ships in the Caribbean.

6. To announce the holiday schedule now would be **to do so before the time is right**.

7. After the flood, the **people who remained alive** returned to their homes to clean away the mud.

8. Alberto had no other **choice open** but to take the test on Friday, even though he was still sick.

9. We did not stay for the **entire time** of the concert because Madelaine was too tired.

10. Lions and tigers are **animals that eat meat**.

3C Applying Meanings

Circle the letter of each correct answer to the questions below. A question may have more than one correct answer.

1. Which of the following would be **optional** on most cars?
   - (a) brakes
   - (b) tires
   - (c) roof rack
   - (d) CD player

2. Which of the following can be **preserved**?
   - (a) freedom
   - (b) fruit
   - (c) letters
   - (d) clouds

3. Which of the following can become **extinct**?
   - (a) languages
   - (b) volcanoes
   - (c) plants
   - (d) animals

4. Which of the following is an **ancestor**?
   - (a) your brother
   - (b) your daughter
   - (c) your great-grandmother
   - (d) your grandson

5. Which of the following are **carnivorous**?
   - (a) wolves
   - (b) rabbits
   - (c) cows
   - (d) frogs

6. Which of the following can be **premature**?
   (a) a death   (c) an announcement
   (b) a holiday   (d) a baby

7. Which of the following might be **ferocious**?
   (a) a polar bear   (c) a hungry dog
   (b) a teddy bear   (d) a hungry baby

8. Which of the following might be hard to **comprehend**?
   (a) a computer game   (c) a foreign language
   (b) a shopping list   (d) a card game

3D Word Study

Many of our English words come to us from Latin. We say they have Latin roots. Our word *liberty*, for example, is formed from the Latin word *liber*, meaning free.

Here are ten Latin words that provide the roots of some English words:

cultus (till)   *trahere* (to draw)   *ferox* (fierce)   *maturus* (fully grown)   *vivere* (to live)
carnis (meat)   *durare* (to last)   *videre* (to see)   *pedester* (on foot)   *prehendere* (grasp)

In the spaces provided, write the Latin word forming the root of each English word together with its meaning.

Definition	English word	Latin word
1. not fully formed	premature	_____
Meaning _____		
2. to stay alive	survive	_____
Meaning _____		
3. meat-eating	carnivore	_____
Meaning _____		
4. with great savagery	ferocious	_____
Meaning _____		
5. one who goes on foot	pedestrian	_____
Meaning _____		
6. to till or work the soil	cultivate	_____
Meaning _____		

ancestor
carnivore
comprehend
duration
evident
extinct
ferocious
gigantic
obscure
option
premature
preserve
prey
puny
survive

7. to draw attention away   distract   _____

Meaning _____

8. to grasp the meaning of   comprehend   _____

Meaning _____

9. the time something lasts   duration   _____

Meaning _____

10. plain to see   evident   _____

Meaning _____

3E Passage

Read the passage below; then complete the exercise that follows.

The Last Dinosaurs

When people think of dinosaurs, the one that comes to mind most frequently is *Tyrannosaurus rex,* a **gigantic** monster almost fifty feet in length and weighing five tons. With curved eight-inch talons on its feet and a huge jaw lined with teeth as long and as sharp as steak knives, it was thought to have been the most terrifying of all the **carnivorous** dinosaurs. Imagine the surprise, then, when scientists digging in eastern Utah in 1992 found **preserved** in the rock the remains of a dinosaur that could well have been a match for *Tyrannosaurus rex.*

Named *Utahraptor,* this **ferocious** creature was "only" twenty feet long, but it had twelve-inch hooked claws on each of its hind legs. Unlike *Tyrannosaurus rex,* which had surprisingly short and **puny** forelimbs, *Utahraptor* had large, powerful arms equipped with ten-inch claws. With these it could grasp its **prey**. Once it had brought its victim down, it could slash with the terrible claws on its hind feet. Nor was flight an **option** for an animal being attacked; with its sturdy back legs *Utahraptor* could probably outrun any other creature. A contest between these two powerful creatures of the dinosaur world never took place, however. All of the *Utahraptors* had been dead for fifty million years before *Tyrannosaurus rex* ever appeared.

It is difficult to **comprehend** the vast stretch of time that dinosaurs lived on the earth—well over a hundred and fifty million years. *Tyrannosaurus rex* was among the last of the dinosaurs; it died out sixty-five million years ago. Human beings have been around for only two or three million years. It will be a long time before we equal the **duration** of the dinosaurs' stay on earth.

No one knows why these creatures became **extinct**, but it seems **evident** from the record left in the earth's crust that it happened fairly suddenly. We know that a meteorite, a large mass of rock or metal from outer space, hit the earth in what is now Mexico about sixty-five million years ago, making a crater almost two hundred miles across. Dust from such an impact would have **obscured** the light from the sun for many weeks and caused freezing temperatures. Much of the earth's plant life would have died, making it difficult for many animals to **survive.**

However, it would be **premature** to say for certain that this was what brought an end to the dinosaurs; scientists are still studying the subject. Indeed, the discovery in China of the bones of *Sinornis,* a feathered dinosaur that perched and flew, has led some scientists to claim that this creature may be the **ancestor** of today's birds. If this turns out to be true, then it would be possible to say that the dinosaurs never died out at all.

Answer each of the following questions in the form of a sentence. If a question does not contain a vocabulary word from this lesson's word list, use one in your answer. Use each word only once. Questions and answers will then contain all fifteen words (or forms of the words).

1. How do scientists know that *Utahraptor* ever lived?

2. What was the **duration** of the age of the dinosaurs?

3. When did the last of the dinosaurs die out?

4. What are some things scientists now **comprehend** about *Utahraptor*?

5. What is the meaning of **prey** as it is used in the passage?

6. How did *Tyrannosaurus rex* compare in size to *Utahraptor*?

7. What is the meaning of **survive** as it is used in the passage?

8. What were the **options** of a creature attacked by *Utahraptor*?

9. Were the forelimbs of *Tyrannosaurus rex* as powerful as those of *Utahraptor*?

10. Why is it **premature** to say for certain what brought an end to the dinosaurs?

11. Did the dinosaurs die out over a long period of time?

12. Why would a meteorite crashing into the earth affect the sunlight?

13. Why do some scientists say a dinosaur may be the **ancestor** of birds?

14. How would you describe the eating habits of *Tyrannosaurus rex* and *Utahraptor*?

15. Why would other creatures probably try to avoid *Utahraptor*?

FUN & FASCINATING FACTS

A **carnivore** is a meat-eating animal, especially a mammal that hunts for its food. Certain plants that eat insects, such as the Venus flytrap, are also *carnivorous*. The word comes from the Latin word *carn,* which means "meat" or "flesh." *Chili con carne* is a Spanish phrase in which the word *carne* comes from the same Latin word; the phrase means "chili with meat."

Things that are hard, such as stone, iron, or bones, are slow to decay or wear away, and so they last a long time. The Romans saw how these two qualities, of being hard and lasting a long time, were related. The Latin words *durus* "hard," and *durare*, "to last a long time" show this connection and form the root of several English words. In addition to **duration**, there is *endure*, which means "to last a long time." In the United States, the separation of church and state is a concept that has *endured* for more than two centuries. *Durable* goods are items such as cars and refrigerators that are expected to last a long time.

Prey and *pray* are homophones, words that sound alike but have different meanings and spellings. To pray means to ask, request, or plead; *pray* can also mean to offer praise, ask for help, or give thanks.

The Latin phrase *puis ne* means "born afterward" and was applied to Roman children of noble birth who followed the firstborn. Since Roman titles and property passed to the oldest, the other children, those who were *puis ne*, were considered to be less powerful. The phrase passed into English as our adjective **puny**.

Lesson 4

Word List Study the definitions of the words below; then do the exercises for the lesson.

accurate
ak´ yər ət

adj. 1. Able to give a correct reading or measurement.
This clock is so **accurate** that it gains less than one second a year.
2. Without mistakes or errors in facts.
In science class we make **accurate** drawings of the plants we study.
accuracy *n.* Correctness, exactness.
I question the **accuracy** of your report because others have described the accident quite differently.

approximate
ə präk´ si mət

adj. Not exact, but close enough to be reasonably correct.
My **approximate** weight is a hundred and ten pounds.

course
kôrs

n. 1. The path over which something moves.
The spaceship is now on a **course** for Mars.
2. A way of acting or behaving.
Because it is raining so hard, our best **course** is to wait in the car until the storm ends.
3. A subject or set of subjects to be studied.
The high school science **course** includes several field trips.

depart
dē pärt´

v. To leave; to go away from a place.
The bus for Detroit **departs** at ten o'clock.
departure *n.* The act of leaving.
We were sad after the **departure** of our friends.

despair
də spâr´

v. To lose hope.
When neither the library nor the bookstore had it, I **despaired** of ever finding the book I wanted.
n. A total lack of hope.
The look of **despair** on their faces told me that the situation was worse than I had feared.

destination
des tə nā´ shən

n. The place to which something or someone is going.
Tell the clerk your **destination** when you buy your ticket.

deteriorate
dē tir´ ē ər āt

v. To make or become worse.
Smoking causes the lungs and heart to **deteriorate**.

gale
gāl

n. 1. A very strong wind.
Last night's **gale** tore several tiles off the roof.
2. A loud outburst.
We heard **gales** of laughter coming from the party.

horizon
hər ī´ zən

n. The apparent line in the distance where the sky meets the sea or land.
We watched the setting sun sink slowly over the **horizon**.
horizontal *adj.* (hər i zänt´ l) Going straight across from side to side.
The shoeboxes were in a **horizontal** row at the back of the closet.

24

jubilation	*n.* A feeling or expression of great joy.
joob bə lā´ shən	There was jubilation among the fans when the Patriots won the 2004 Super Bowl.
	jubilant *adj.* (joob´ bə lənt) Very happy.
	My family was **jubilant** when Aunt Jean survived the heart operation.

navigate	*v.* To calculate or direct the movement of a ship or aircraft.
nav´ ə gāt	Phoenician sailors **navigated** by measuring the position of the sun and stars.
	navigation *n.* The science or practice of navigating.
	Clocks and sextants are instruments used in **navigation**.

nostalgia	*n.* A longing for a certain time in the past.
näs tal´ jə	Seeing the photographs of my first dog filled me with **nostalgia**.
	nostalgic *adj.* Having feelings of nostalgia.
	I became **nostalgic** when I heard you playing the song my grandfather used to sing to me.

revive	*v.* 1. To make or become strong again.
rē vīv´	A short rest will **revive** you.
	2. To bring back into use or fashion.
	The show **revives** a number of songs from the fifties.

sever	*v.* 1. To break off.
sev´ ər	When the plane that crashed was proven to be on a spy mission, the two countries **severed** all ties with each other.
	2. To cut in two.
	Irving accidentally **severed** the garden hose while mowing the lawn.

voyage	*n.* A long journey by sea or in space.
voi´ ij	The **voyage** across the Pacific will take three weeks.
	v. To make a journey by sea or in space.
	Long before Columbus, the Vikings **voyaged** across the Atlantic Ocean to reach North America.

4A Finding Meanings

Choose two phrases to form a sentence that correctly uses a word from Word List 4. Write each sentence in the space provided.

1. (a) get worse.
   (b) To deteriorate is to
   (c) To revive is to
   (d) feel slightly uneasy.

2. (a) An accurate account is
   (b) one that is obscure.
   (c) A jubilant account is
   (d) one that is without errors.

3. (a) make it strong again.
   (b) To sever a friendship is to
   (c) To revive a friendship is to
   (d) look back on it with fond memories.

4. (a) A destination is   (c) a setting out from a place.
   (b) A course is   (d) the path over which something moves.

5. (a) Something that is horizontal   (c) is falling into a state of disrepair.
   (b) is not exact.   (d) Something that is approximate

6. (a) the act of leaving.   (c) A destination is
   (b) A departure is   (d) a long journey by sea.

7. (a) a lack of understanding.   (c) Nostalgia is
   (b) a feeling of longing for the past.   (d) Despair is

8. (a) A voyage is   (c) a strong wind.
   (b) a small boat.   (d) A gale is

9. (a) Jubilation is   (c) the directing of a ship's movement.
   (b) Navigation is   (d) the length of time something lasts.

10. (a) To despair is to   (c) return to one's starting point.
   (b) To voyage is to   (d) feel a sense of hopelessness.

accurate
approximate
course
depart
despair
destination
deteriorate
gale
horizon
jubilation
navigate
nostalgia
revive
sever
voyage

4B Just the Right Word

Improve each of the following sentences by crossing out the bold phrase and replacing it with a word (or a form of the word) from Word List 4.

1. The **loud outbursts** of laughter from the next room distracted me from my work.

2. I will be responsible for **working out the direction the boat should be headed** when we sail to Bali.

3. The **place to which it is going** is shown on the front of the bus.

4. We **start on our journey** at ten o'clock tomorrow morning.

5. The ship met with stormy weather during the **long journey by sea** around Cape Horn.

6. Early this morning the **apparent line where the sky and sea meet** was obscured by the fog.

7. When the driver told me that the bus ride to Boston would take two hours, my friend said that was **close enough to be almost correct**.

8. Each **set of subjects to be studied** takes one year to complete.

9. I **completely broke off** my relationship with the company when I got a new job.

10. Nina and her best friend were **filled with joy** when they were assigned to the same tent.

4C Applying Meanings

Circle the letter of each correct answer to the questions below. A question may have more than one correct answer.

1. Which of the following can **depart**?
   - (a) a train
   - (b) a ship
   - (c) a guest
   - (d) a noise

2. Which of the following could you **sever**?
   - (a) a branch of a tree
   - (b) a puff of smoke
   - (c) a relationship
   - (d) a finger

3. Which of the following could be a **destination**?
   - (a) a town in the Midwest
   - (b) a friendship
   - (c) next Tuesday
   - (d) Hollywood

4. Which of the following is a **course**?
   - (a) the earth's path around the sun
   - (b) taking a wait-and-see attitude
   - (c) "Introduction to Science"
   - (d) the start of a race

5. On which of the following might you **voyage**?
   - (a) an ocean liner
   - (b) the space shuttle
   - (c) a rowboat
   - (d) a helicopter

6. Which of the following might make a person feel **nostalgic**?
   - (a) thinking about the past
   - (b) making plans for the future
   - (c) looking at old photographs
   - (d) meeting an old friend

7. Which of the following can be **accurate**?
   - (a) a clock
   - (b) a statement
   - (c) a drawing
   - (d) a weather forecast

8. Which of the following can be **navigated**?

(a) a spaceship   (c) a train

(b) an airplane   (d) a boat

4D Word Study

Look at each group of four words below. If you think two of the words in a group are synonyms, circle those words and write *S* in the space next to the words.

If you think two of the words in a group are antonyms, circle those words and write *A* in the space next to the words.

1. cluster	navigate	deteriorate	improve	_____
2. nostalgia	distraction	jubilation	joy	_____
3. obvious	evident	equivalent	extinct	_____
4. depart	cultivate	arrive	retire	_____
5. puny	burly	nostalgic	grateful	_____
6. brittle	patient	correct	accurate	_____
7. navigate	comprehend	understand	arrive	_____
8. sever	preserve	save	obscure	_____
9. separate	hold	forget	combine	_____
10. patience	jubilation	despair	duration	_____

4E Passage

Read the passage below; then complete the exercise that follows.

accurate

approximate

course

depart

despair

destination

deteriorate

gale

horizon

jubilation

navigate

nostalgia

revive

sever

voyage

A Difficult Journey

In England in the early seventeenth century, people were not free to worship as they pleased. This was a matter decided for them by the government, and those who did not like this could leave. So it was that on September 6, 1620, a sailing ship called the *Mayflower* **departed** from Plymouth, England, with a hundred and two passengers.

Many of those on board were leaving in order to be free to worship in their own way. Later, they were called Pilgrims, the name for people who make long journeys because of a deep religious faith. Others on the ship were simply hoping to make a new life for themselves in America. The passengers, however, did not want to **sever** all ties with England. They had to pay back the money they had borrowed to make this journey, and they intended to do this by trading with the old country.

The *Mayflower's* **destination** was Virginia, where others from England had settled thirteen years before. But getting there was no simple matter. In those days, when sailors were out of sight of land, they **navigated** by measuring the position of the sun and stars. When the sun told them it was noon, the clocks on board gave a different time, depending on how far east or west they had traveled. The difference in time was used to calculate their position. But their clocks and other instruments were not very **accurate**, and when clouds obscured the sun or stars, figuring out where they were and in what direction they were headed was not easy.

For the first couple of weeks of the *Mayflower's* **voyage**, gentle breezes carried the ship along, and the passengers sat on deck and enjoyed the sunshine. Later on, however, the weather **deteriorated**. Strong **gales** rocked the *Mayflower* and made life miserable for the passengers; many people became sick. One person died and was buried at sea. A woman named Elizabeth Hopkins had a baby in mid-ocean and named the child Oceanus. Day after day, the Pilgrims stared at the **horizon**, hoping for the sight of land to **revive** their spirits. Day after day, all they saw was endless sea and sky. Many **despaired** of ever reaching America. Then at last, after sixty-five days, they saw land. That day there was great **jubilation** on board the *Mayflower*.

The Pilgrims soon discovered, however, that they had been blown far off their proper **course** by strong winds in the mid-Atlantic. Instead of landing in Virginia, they found themselves on Cape Cod, **approximately** five hundred miles to the north. For several weeks they explored the coast of Cape Cod Bay, looking for a place in which to settle. They had little time because the bitterly cold winter weather was almost upon them.

Finally, in late December, they discovered a suitable spot. the passengers went ashore to plan the new settlement and build houses. The place where they landed had been visited earlier by English explorers, and the name they had given it may have made some of the Pilgrims **nostalgic**. It was called Plymouth.

Answer each of the following questions in the form of a sentence. If a question does not contain a vocabulary word from this lesson's word list, use one in your answer. Use each word only once. Questions and answers will then contain all fifteen words (or forms of the words).

1. What option was open to people in England who wanted to practice their own religion?

_____

2. What is the meaning of **sever** as it is used in the passage?

_____

3. How long did it take the *Mayflower* to get from England to Cape Cod?

_____

4. Where did those on board the *Mayflower* intend to land?

_____

5. What is the meaning of **accurate** as it is used in the passage?

_____

6. **Approximately** how many passengers were there on the *Mayflower*?

_____

7. When did the weather start to get worse?

_____

8. When might it have been dangerous for passengers to go on deck?

9. Why did many passengers **despair** of reaching America?

10. What problem would cloudy skies cause for the crew of the *Mayflower?*

11. Where did the passengers first see land?

12. What is the meaning of **revive** as it is used in the passage?

13. How might the religious Pilgrims have expressed their **jubilation** at seeing land?

14. Name some of the things that the Pilgrims might have felt **nostalgia** for.

15. What **course** was open to the Pilgrims when they found themselves on Cape Cod instead of in Virginia?

FUN & FASCINATING FACTS

Don't confuse **course**, a noun that has several meanings, with the adjective *coarse,* which means "rough to the touch; crude; not fine." These two words are homophones; they are pronounced the same but have different meanings and spellings.

Winds have different names, depending on the speed at which they blow. A *breeze* goes from 4 miles per hour (a light breeze) to 31 m.p.h. (a strong breeze). A **gale** has a wind speed of from 32 to 63 m.p.h. A *storm* is a wind blowing between 64 and 73 m.p.h. A *hurricane* has a wind speed of over 74 m.p.h.

Both **revive** and *survive* (Word List 3) come from the Latin word *vivus,* which means "living, alive."

Review for Lessons 1–4

Hidden Message In the spaces provided to the right of each sentence, write the vocabulary words from Lessons 1 through 4 that are missing in each of the sentences below. Be sure that the words you choose fit the meaning of each sentence and have the same number of letters as there are spaces. The number following each sentence gives the lesson from which the missing word comes. If the exercise is done correctly, the shaded boxes will spell out the answer to this riddle:

How can mail carriers tell how many letters there are in a mailbox without looking inside?

1. I don't let anything _____ me while I'm working. (1)

2. A(n) _____ of mine fought in the Civil War. (3)

3. Cats _____ on mice, chipmunks, and birds. (3)

4. The bus's _____ was New York City. (4)

5. The dog looks _____, but it's quite harmless. (3)

6. Your eyes will soon _____ themselves to the dark. (1)

7. My parents hope to _____ a new car this year. (2)

8. The tires on the earth mover were _____. (3)

9. We have no other _____ but to continue. (3)

10. The _____ was admitted to the hospital this morning. (1)

11. A(n) _____ dog does not have to be told twice. (1)

12. If I _____ this storm, I'm never going sailing again. (3)

13. Last night's _____ blew several tiles off the roof. (4)

14. My _____ on the trip was an old school friend. (1)

15. The speck on the _____ turned out to be an island. (4)

16. I refused to _____ when told to give up my seat. (1)

17. A drink and a short rest will soon _____ us. (4)

18. Give me the _____ day of your arrival. (4)

19. The director will _____ you to your new section. (1)

20. Those trees _____ the view of the lake. (3)

21. Are you and your roommate _____? (1)

22. A large _____ of grapes hung from the vine. (2)

23. The _____ from Seattle to Sidney took a month. (4)

24. A single blow from an axe will _____ the rope. (4)

25. You can _____ mushrooms in any dark, damp place. (2)

26. We will _____ by the stars on our ocean crossing. (4)

27. I felt a sudden wave of _____ for the good old days. (4)

28. A driver needs to be _____ at all times. (1)

29. Do you _____ the meaning of the message? (3)

30. I plan to _____ early as I have to be up at six. (1)

31. Candy canes are very _____, so don't drop any. (2)

32. The _____ we had to follow was laid out for us. (4)

33. I went up and said, "Allow me to _____ myself." (2)

34. You can _____ peaches by canning them. (3)

35. The tiger is a(n) _____ and eats only meat. (3)

36. I'm trying to cut down on the fats that I _____. (2)

37. The Rockies were a(n) _____ to those heading west. (1)

38. The _____ of popcorn made our mouths water. (2)

39. What is the _____ of a dollar in Mexican money? (2)

40. Leather will _____ if it is not properly cared for. (4)

41. I felt someone in the crowd _____ me. (1)

42. Two _____ men piled the wood in the truck. (1)

43. Sam cannot understand the _____ of a budget. (1)

44. We _____ grain to many countries. (2)

Lesson 5

Word List
Study the definitions of the words below; then do the exercises for the lesson.

avalanche
av´ ə lanch

n. 1. A great mass of ice, earth, or snow mixed with rocks sliding down a mountain.
The mountain climbers had a narrow escape when the **avalanche** swept over them.
2. A great amount of something.
Our company had an **avalanche** of orders after we used a television ad for our new game.

blizzard
bliz´ ərd

n. A heavy snowstorm with strong winds.
The Chicago airport had to close for two days because of the **blizzard**.

challenge
chal´ ənj

v. 1. To invite others to take part in a contest.
I **challenged** my friend to a game of chess.
2. To cause a person to use a lot of skill or effort.
This trail **challenges** even the best skiers.
3. To question or to argue against, especially when something is unfair or unjust.
Very few scientists **challenge** the idea that a large meteorite killed off the last of the dinosaurs sixty-five million years ago.
n. 1. An interesting task or problem; something that takes skill or effort.
Living out of our backpacks for a week on the mountain was a real **challenge**.
2. A call to take part in a contest.
I accepted the **challenge** to run in the marathon.

conquer
käŋ´ kər

v. 1. To get the better of.
Swimming lessons at the YMCA helped me to **conquer** my fear of the water.
2. To defeat.
Hannibal's army **conquered** part of Spain in 219 B.C.
conquest *n.* The act of defeating.
The Norman **conquest** of England took place in 1066.

crevice
krev´ is

n. A deep, narrow opening in rock caused by a split or crack.
The **crevice** had filled with soil in which a cluster of small red flowers was growing.

foolhardy
fool´ här dē

adj. Unwisely bold or daring.
It would be **foolhardy** to go sailing during a gale.

lure
loor

v. To tempt or attract with the promise of something good.
In the early nineteenth century, the hope of owning land of their own **lured** many people to travel west to Ohio and Indiana.
n. 1. Something that attracts.
The **lure** of the sea led us to take up sailing.
2. Artificial bait used for fishing.
A large striped bass took the **lure**, and I hooked it.

makeshift
māk´ shift

n. A temporary and usually less strong replacement.
They used the trailer as a **makeshift** while their house was being rebuilt.
adj. Used as a temporary replacement.
We use the sofa as a **makeshift** bed when we have overnight guests.

optimist
äp´ tə mist

n. One who looks at things in the most positive way; a cheerful, hopeful person.
Pat and Jean are **optimists** and so, of course, they believed the plane would not leave without us.
optimistic *adj.* Cheerful; hopeful.
In spite of the injuries to our best players, I am **optimistic** about our chances of winning the big game.
optimism *n.* A feeling of hope or cheerfulness.
The patients' **optimism** helped them recover more quickly from their illnesses.

previous
prē´ vē əs

adj. Earlier; happening before.
Although I missed the last meeting, I attended the two **previous** ones.

route
rōōt

n. 1. The path that must be followed to get to a place.
Our **route** to Seattle takes us through Denver.
2. A fixed course or area assigned to a sales or delivery person.
Magali has over a hundred customers on her newspaper **route**.

summit
sum´ it

n. 1. The highest part; the top.
It took us three hours to climb to the **summit** of Mount Washington.
2. A conference or meeting of the top leaders of governments.
The **summit** of African heads of state will take place in Nairobi in late June.

terse
tûrs

adj. Short and to the point.
When I said I was sure we would be rescued soon, my friend's **terse** reply was, "How?"

thwart
thwôrt

v. To block or defeat the plans or efforts of.
Heavy fighting **thwarted** the UN's attempts to deliver food.

vertical
vʉrt´ i kəl

adj. Running straight up and down; upright.
The black **vertical** lines in this painting are what one notices first.

5A Finding Meanings

Choose two phrases to form a sentence that correctly uses a word from Word List 5. Write each sentence in the space provided.

1. (a) the way to reach the top.
   (b) a meeting of heads of state.
   (c) A lure is
   (d) A summit is

2. (a) An optimistic statement is one
   (b) that is released to the public.
   (c) A previous statement is one
   (d) that was made earlier.

3. (a) To lure someone is
   (b) To thwart someone is
   (c) to offer help or advice to that person.
   (d) to tempt that person with promises.

4. (a) an area assigned to a salesperson.   (c) a payment for something done.
   (b) A crevice is   (d) A route is

5. (a) To be thwarted is to be   (c) prevented from carrying out one's plans.
   (b) To be challenged is to be   (d) attracted by promises.

6. (a) An optimistic report is one   (c) that is written out.
   (b) that is hopeful.   (d) A terse report is one

7. (a) a call to take part in a contest.   (c) A challenge is
   (b) a severe snowstorm with high winds.   (d) An avalanche is

8. (a) A makeshift file is one that   (c) stores things upright.
   (b) A vertical file is one that   (d) gets narrower toward the top.

9. (a) A foolhardy remark is one   (c) that sounds threatening.
   (b) that is short and to the point.   (d) A terse remark is one

10. (a) a split or crack in rock.   (c) A blizzard is
    (b) a mass of falling rocks and snow.   (d) An avalanche is

avalanche
blizzard
challenge
conquer
crevice
foolhardy
lure
makeshift
optimist
previous
route
summit
terse
thwart
vertical

5B Just the Right Word

Improve each of the following sentences by crossing out the bold phrase and replacing it with a word (or a form of the word) from Word List 5.

1. Your **daring but unwise** leap off the boat almost cost you your life.

2. What kind of **artificial bait** is best for catching bluefish?

3. Being appointed chairman of the Joint Chiefs of Staff was the **highest point** of General Colin Powell's military career.

4. According to the radio, we can expect a **severe snowstorm with very strong winds** tonight.

5. I'm driving to Yellowstone this summer and wonder which would be the best **way to get there**.

6. The German army's **defeat of the armed forces** of France in 1940 took less than four weeks.

7. A **deep, narrow opening made by a split in the rock** provided a toehold for the climbers making their way up the cliff face.

8. Swimming across the lake will be quite a **difficult task requiring great skill and effort**.

9. What is the reason for Gail's **feeling that all will go well**?

10. Bruno didn't have a pillow, so he used a rolled-up coat as a **temporary replacement for one** and slept quite soundly.

5C Applying Meanings

Circle the letter of each correct answer to the questions below. A question may have more than one correct answer.

1. Which of the following might an optimist say?
   (a) "Things could be a lot worse!"
   (b) "Don't count your chickens."
   (c) "What's the use?"
   (d) "I know we can do it."

2. Which of the following might be a lure to a person?
   (a) the Broadway stage
   (b) the presidency
   (c) an ocean voyage
   (d) a tropical island

3. Which of the following might challenge a person?
   (a) competing in the Olympics
   (b) watching a TV show
   (c) driving a racing car
   (d) reading a comic book

4. Of which of the following could there be an avalanche?
   (a) letters
   (b) orders
   (c) gales
   (d) requests

5. Which of the following would you expect to be vertical?
   (a) a sleeping person
   (b) a front door
   (c) the horizon
   (d) a stairway

6. Which of the following might thwart someone?
   (a) support from a friend
   (b) a sudden change in the weather
   (c) a flat tire
   (d) lack of money

7. Which of the following is foolhardy?

    (a) skating on thin ice   (c) losing your wallet

    (b) riding a horse   (d) eating salad

8. Which of the following can be terse?

    (a) a comment   (c) a phone conversation

    (b) muscles   (d) an aroma

5D Word Study

A *prefix* is the part of a word that comes at the beginning. The part that comes at the end is called a *suffix*. One of the things a suffix does is change a word from one part of speech to another. The *-ive* ending changes the verb *create* into the adjective *creative*. The *-or* ending changes it into the noun *creator*.

Turn the following verbs into nouns by adding the suffix *-ment, -(t)ion, -ing,* or *-or.*

1. assign   _____

2. distract   _____

3. combine   _____

4. crave   _____

5. survive   _____

Turn the following nouns into adjectives by adding the suffix *-ic, -al,* or *-ous.*

6. optimist   _____

7. horizon   _____

8. nostalgia   _____

9. ferocity   _____

10. carnivore _____

Turn the following adjectives into nouns by adding the suffix *-cy, -(t)ion,* or *-ence.*

11. accurate   _____

12. jubilant   _____

13. navigate   _____

14. obedient   _____

15. patient   _____

avalanche
blizzard
challenge
conquer
crevice
foolhardy
lure
makeshift
optimist
previous
route
summit
terse
thwart
vertical

5E Passage

Read the passage below; then complete the exercise that follows.

On Top of the World

The world's greatest climbers have always been drawn to Mount Everest, but in trying to climb it, many have been **lured** to their deaths. Located on the border of two Asian countries, Nepal and Tibet, Everest is part of the Himalayan mountain chain north of India. It is just over twenty-nine thousand feet high. Other mountains are more difficult to climb and offer a greater **challenge**, but because it is the world's highest mountain, Everest has a special place in our imaginations.

Every attempt to reach the top requires careful planning and can cost over a quarter of a million dollars. Often climbers hire Nepalese guides called Sherpas, who are skilled and experienced mountaineers. Together they work out the **route** to take and set up camps along the way.

Because the air is so thin near the top, climbers need to bring oxygen with them, adding greatly to the weight that must be carried. In recent years, small groups of climbers have made attempts on Everest without oxygen and without relying on Sherpas. Their daring method has been to travel fast and light and to stay in temporary shelters as they make their way up and down.

Where the mountain rises **vertically**, climbers drive spikes into **crevices** in the rock and pull each other up with ropes. They must be very careful because a loose stone or even a loud noise can start an **avalanche**, burying those who are caught in its path or sweeping them to their deaths. In addition, climbers must be alert to the weather because it can change suddenly for the worse. **Blizzards** often strike with little warning, forcing climbers to scramble for **makeshift** shelter until the danger has passed.

The first people to reach the top of Mount Everest were Edmund Hillary of New Zealand and Tenzing Norgay, his Sherpa guide, in 1953. Teams of mountaineers had made at least eight **previous** tries; but all of them had been **thwarted** in their attempts to stand on the highest spot on earth, some by bad planning, some by bad weather, some by bad luck. The first woman to **conquer** Mount Everest was Junko Tabei, of Japan, in 1975; the first American woman to do so was Stacy Allison, in 1988.

Mountaineers are by nature **optimists**. They want to believe they will be able to reach the top. At times, however, if either their physical condition or the weather is deteriorating, they are forced to ask themselves if it would be **foolhardy** to continue. Their state of mind plays a big part in this decision, which must sometimes be made when they are only a few hundred feet from the **summit**. Many have chosen to continue, a decision that cost them their lives.

By 2001, just under fifteen hundred people had succeeded in climbing to the top of Mount Everest, but almost a hundred and fifty had died in the attempt. Why do it if it is so difficult and so dangerous? Someone once put this question to the English climber George Mallory, who made several unsuccessful tries to climb Mount Everest and died there with less than six hundred feet to go, in 1924, on what became his last attempt. He gave the **terse** reply, "Because it's there."

Answer each of the following questions in the form of a sentence. If a question does not contain a vocabulary word from this lesson's word list, use one in your answer. Use each word only once. Questions and answers will then contain all fifteen words (or forms of the words).

1. What would you think of someone who planned to climb Mount Everest alone?

2. What is the meaning of **challenge** as it is used in the passage?

3. Why would it be unwise to blow an airhorn while high up on Mount Everest?

4. Why would you expect conversations between climbers to be **terse**?

5. Why do climbers watch the weather carefully?

6. What weather conditions would make a mountain climber **optimistic**?

7. How are **crevices** useful to climbers?

8. What is the meaning of **route** as it is used in the passage?

9. What should people do if caught in bad weather while climbing a mountain?

10. When do climbers need to use ropes?

11. What would happen to a team of climbers who couldn't raise enough money for an attempt on Mount Everest?

12. How did George Mallory explain the **lure** of Mount Everest?

13. Why would Mallory have been familiar with Everest on his last climb?

14. How do you suppose climbers know when they have reached the **summit**?

15. Why would climbers feel **jubilant** while standing on the top of Everest?

FUN & FASCINATING FACTS

Until 1881, a **blizzard** was a loud noise or blast. In that year the *New York Nation* said: "The hard weather has called into use a word which promises to become a national Americanism, namely *blizzard*. It [is the word for] a storm of snow and wind which we cannot resist away from shelter." That is how the word came to have its present meaning. To be called a blizzard, a storm must have winds above thirty-five miles an hour, a temperature close to zero, blowing snow that reduces visibility, and lasts at least three hours.

The antonym of **optimist** is *pessimist*. Imagine two people looking at a glass of water. The *optimist* thinks the glass is half full; the *pessimist* thinks it is half empty.

Route is sometimes pronounced ROOT and sometimes ROWT; both are correct. Don't confuse this word with *rout*, also pronounced ROWT, which means "a total and complete defeat." *Route* and *root* can be homophones (when both are pronounced ROOT), and so can *route* and *rout* (when both are pronounced ROWT).

Vertical and *horizontal* (Word List 4) are antonyms. In a crossword puzzle the *horizontal* answers must fit perfectly with the *vertical* answers.

Lesson 6

Word List Study the definitions of the words below; then do the exercises for the lesson.

abolish
ə bäl´ ish

v. To bring to an end; to do away with.
Most people would support a plan to **abolish** weapons of mass destruction.

agony
ag´ ə nē

n. Great pain of mind or body; suffering.
The pinched nerve caused him **agony** for several weeks.
agonizing *adj.* (ag´ ə nīz iŋ) Very painful.
Watching their sick child in the hospital bed was **agonizing** to the parents.

catapult
kat´ ə pult

n. A machine used in ancient wars that threw objects with great force.
Roman **catapults** could throw six-pound objects almost a third of a mile.
v. To move or be moved suddenly and with great force, as if by a catapult.
The Groaners' latest song **catapulted** them to the top of the country music charts.

character
kər´ ək tər

n. 1. The qualities that make a person or place different or special.
Your friend's support during your long illness demonstrates her true **character**.
2. A person in a story, movie, or play.
Madame Defarge and Sydney Carton are the two **characters** I remember most clearly from *A Tale of Two Cities*.
3. A letter or symbol used in writing or printing.
The license plate number NKT605 contains six **characters**.

denounce
dē nouns´

v. 1. To speak out against something; to criticize.
The president **denounced** Congress for failing to approve the budget.
2. To accuse someone of doing wrong.
Carla **denounced** Victor, who sat next to her, for cheating on the test.

escalate
es´ kə lāt

v. To go up or increase in size or scope.
If house prices continue to **escalate**, many people will be unable to afford to buy a home.

grim
grim

adj. 1. Cruel; fierce.
There were many **grim** battles during the Civil War.
2. Unfriendly or threatening; stern.
The coach's **grim** face expressed his displeasure at our team's poor performance.
3. Unpleasant; disturbing.
We heard the **grim** news that no one had survived the plane crash.

harbor
här´ bər

n. A protected place along a seacoast where ships can find shelter.
In the summer the **harbor** is busy with sailboats going in and out.
v. 1. To give shelter to; to take care of by hiding.
In most states, it is a crime to **harbor** someone wanted by the police.
2. To hold and nourish a thought or feeling in the mind.
Try not to **harbor** anger against the person who stole your bike.

inflict in flikt´	*v.* To cause something painful to be felt. The hurricane **inflicted** severe damage on coastal areas.
loathe lōth	*v.* To hate or dislike greatly. Mahatma Gandhi, the great Indian leader, **loathed** violence. **loathing** *n.* A feeling of hatred. Their **loathing** of cruelty to animals led them to set up a shelter for unwanted pets.
meddle med´ əl	*v.* To involve oneself in other people's affairs without being asked. When my grandparents retired, they could have **meddled** in my parents' lives, but they didn't. **meddlesome** *adj.* Given to taking part in others' affairs without being asked. If you think I am being **meddlesome**, just tell me to mind my own business.
monstrous män´ strəs	*adj.* 1. Causing shock; horrible; wicked. Hitler's **monstrous** plan to murder the Jews of Europe was carried out in concentration camps in Germany and Poland. 2. Extremely large. A **monstrous** statue of the Soviet leader Joseph Stalin, three times life-size, stood in the town square.
rouse rouz	*v.* 1. To awaken, to wake up. The children were sleeping so soundly that it was difficult to **rouse** them. 2. To stir up; to excite. Martin Luther King, Jr., **roused** the American people with his 1963 speech at the Lincoln Memorial, in Washington, D.C.
steadfast sted´ fast	*adj.* Unchanging; steady; loyal. Rigo and Moni remained **steadfast** friends throughout their school years.
translate trans lāt´	*v.* To put into a different language. *The Little Prince*, which was written in French, was **translated** into English by Katherine Woods.

6A Finding Meanings

Choose two phrases to form a sentence that correctly uses a word from Word List 6. Write each sentence in the space provided.

1. (a) involve oneself in the affairs of others.
   (b) hold certain thoughts in the mind.
   (c) To translate is to
   (d) To meddle is to

2. (a) A harbor is something that
   (b) is expressed in another language.
   (c) hurls objects with great force.
   (d) A catapult is something that

3. (a) feels resentment against others.   (c) A monstrous person is one who
   (b) is not easily changed by others.   (d) A steadfast person is one who

4. (a) To loathe something is to   (c) express it in a different language.
   (b) To translate something is to   (d) present it for the first time.

5. (a) one that is very wicked.   (c) one that keeps getting put off.
   (b) An agonizing decision is   (d) A monstrous decision is

6. (a) a protected place for boats.   (c) A harbor is
   (b) anything that shocks or horrifies.   (d) A character is

7. (a) To rouse someone is to   (c) wake up that person.
   (b) say that person's name out loud.   (d) To denounce someone is to

8. (a) a person's special qualities.   (c) deliberate rudeness.
   (b) Character is   (d) Agony is

9. (a) find its causes.   (c) say that it is wrong.
   (b) To denounce a quarrel is to   (d) To escalate a quarrel is to

10. (a) To loathe something is to   (c) To abolish something is to
    (b) have an understanding of it.   (d) feel hatred for it.

abolish

agony

catapult

character

denounce

escalate

grim

harbor

inflict

loathe

meddle

monstrous

rouse

steadfast

translate

6B Just the Right Word

Improve each of the following sentences by crossing out the bold phrase and replacing it with a word (or a form of the word) from Word List 6.

1. Overnight, someone had put up a **gigantic and very unattractive** billboard across the street.

2. Americans in 1776 were **stirred into action** by Thomas Paine's writings.

3. I was in **very great pain** after I fell and twisted my ankle.

4. The school **did away with** the rules that prevented girls from playing on the baseball team.

5. Ida still **holds on to** feelings of mistrust toward Fern, who made promises she knew she could not keep.

6. The **people written about** in Judy Blume's books seem like real people to me.

7. The burned-out buildings were a **disturbing and unpleasant** sign that the city had been under attack.

8. The quarrel between us **became more and more serious**, until we no longer spoke to each other.

9. The Beatles were **suddenly lifted** to world fame in the early 1960s.

10. The 1994 earthquake **was the cause of** heavy damage throughout much of Los Angeles.

6C Applying Meanings

Circle the letter of each correct answer to the questions below. A question may have more than one correct answer.

1. Which of the following might be **denounced**?
   - (a) a plane's arrival
   - (b) a scoundrel
   - (c) an act of cruelty
   - (d) a bad law

2. Which of the following can be **harbored**?
   - (a) anger
   - (b) a car
   - (c) a runaway child
   - (d) hatred

3. Which of the following can be **abolished**?
   - (a) a rule
   - (b) an idea
   - (c) a law
   - (d) a custom

4. Which of the following might **meddlesome** persons do?
   - (a) keep to themselves
   - (b) offer advice freely
   - (c) ask a lot of questions
   - (d) mind their own business

5. Which of the following can be **translated**?
   - (a) paintings
   - (b) music
   - (c) books
   - (d) laughter

6. Which of the following is a **character**?

    (a) Snow White   (c) 9

    (b) &   (d) optimism

7. Which of the following can be **grim**?

    (a) news   (c) weather

    (b) jubilation   (d) vegetables

8. Which of the following could be **agonizing**?

    (a) a bad toothache   (c) a persistent cold

    (b) the death of a friend   (d) a distraction

6D Word Study

Write the synonym of each of the words on the left below in the space next to it. Choose from the words on the right, which are in a different order.

1. conquer   _____   remove

2. sever   _____   hatred

3. obscure   _____   correct

4. extract   _____   stern

5. accurate   _____   short

6. steadfast   _____   defeat

7. loathing   _____   weak

8. grim   _____   cut

9. terse   _____   loyal

10. puny   _____   unclear

abolish

agony

catapult

character

denounce

escalate

grim

harbor

inflict

loathe

meddle

monstrous

rouse

steadfast

translate

6E Passage

Read the passage below; then complete the exercise that follows.

The Pen Is Mightier Than the Sword

In the early nineteenth century, a number of Americans supported slavery, a practice that had been widely accepted since ancient times. Even people who **loathed** slavery, and there were a great many, thought that there was little that one person could do about it. They were wrong. Harriet Beecher Stowe, who was born in Litchfield, Connecticut, in 1811, was someone who caused important changes. She believed that slavery was a **monstrous** crime. While living in Ohio in the 1840s, she used her house to **harbor** slaves who had escaped from their southern owners and were making their way north to freedom. In 1850, after moving to Maine with her minister husband, she wrote a novel called *Uncle Tom's Cabin,* which not only awakened people to the horrors of slavery but also **catapulted** her to world fame.

Her book painted a **grim** picture of slave life. Readers shared the **agony** that the slave mother Eliza felt when she accidentally overheard that her only child was to be sold to a slave trader. They eagerly followed Eliza's adventures after she escaped with her child, crossing the half-frozen Ohio River by jumping from one broken piece of ice to the next, with armed men and yelping dogs close behind. They breathed a sigh of relief when Eliza and her child reached Canada and freedom.

Another **character** in the book is the wise and kindly slave, Uncle Tom. He was sold to Simon Legree, a man who took pleasure in **inflicting** severe punishment on his slaves. When Legree ordered Uncle Tom to give a whipping to a sick and weak female slave who had failed to pick enough cotton, Tom refused. So Legree had him whipped instead. Later, when Uncle Tom **steadfastly** refused to tell Legree where two of his runaway slaves were hiding, Legree had him beaten so severely that he died. Readers wept.

Uncle Tom's Cabin sold millions of copies and was **translated** into many different languages. It was also made into a play that was performed all over the world. The book helped **rouse** the people of America, especially those in the North, into demanding an end to slavery. Of course, not everyone looked with favor on *Uncle Tom's Cabin.* It was banned in the South, and slave owners and their supporters accused Harriet Beecher Stowe of **meddling** in their lives. She ignored their protests and continued to **denounce** slavery in speeches, articles, and books.

The quarrel between North and South over the question of slavery **escalated**. In 1863, in the middle of the Civil War, President Abraham Lincoln signed an order **abolishing** slavery in states then under Confederate control. Harriet Beecher Stowe's novel played no small part in bringing about the war that ended slavery. Her life shows that just one determined person can make a difference.

Answer each of the following questions in the form of a sentence. If a question does not contain a vocabulary word from this lesson's word list, use one in your answer. Use each word only once. Questions and answers will then contain all fifteen words (or forms of the words).

1. What differing views did Americans have of slavery?

2. What happened to the quarrel between North and South over slavery?

3. What event occurred thirteen years after *Uncle Tom's Cabin* was written?

4. Why did Harriet Beecher Stowe suddenly become famous?

5. Which act described in the passage do you think is the most **monstrous**?

6. Why were some people who didn't know English able to read *Uncle Tom's Cabin*?

7. Why is it inaccurate to describe Harriet Beecher Stowe as **meddlesome**?

8. How did Harriet Beecher Stowe stand up to the supporters of slavery?

9. What is the meaning of **character** as it is used in the passage?

10. Why do you think Harriet Beecher Stowe wrote *Uncle Tom's Cabin*?

11. What is the meaning of **harbor** as it is used in the passage?

12. How would you say Eliza's **agony** differed from Uncle Tom's?

13. What is it about Simon Legree that makes him so unpleasant?

14. How did Uncle Tom answer when Simon Legree demanded to know where the runaway slaves were hiding?

15. What is the meaning of **grim** as it is used in the passage?

FUN & FASCINATING FACTS

Two nouns are formed from the verb **abolish.** *Abolition* is the act of abolishing or the state of being abolished. (It took a terrible civil war to bring about the *abolition* of slavery in America.) An *abolitionist* is a person who worked to bring about an end to slavery. (William Lloyd Garrison was a famous *abolitionist* who, for thirty-five years, fought to end slavery in America.)

Don't confuse the verb **loathe** (with a final -e) with the adjective *loath* (without the final -e) which means "unwilling." (We were having such a good time that we were *loath* to leave.) The *th* sound in *loathe* is pronounced as in *then;* the *th* sound in *loath* is pronounced as in *thin.*

The homophones **meddle** and *medal* sound alike but have different meanings and spellings. A medal is a small, flat piece of metal given as an honor or to reward bravery.

The Latin prefix *trans-* means "across" and helps to form many English words. A *transatlantic* voyage is one made across the Atlantic Ocean. A radio or television tower *transmits* signals across the land to be picked up by radio and television sets.

The Latin root *latus* means "to carry" or "to move." It combines with the prefix *trans-* to form **translate**. To translate something is to "move it across" from one language to another.

Lesson 7

> **Word List** Study the definitions of the words below; then do the exercises for the lesson.

colony
käl´ ə nē

n. 1. A group of people, animals, or plants living close together.
We found a **colony** of ants in the yard.
2. A group of people who settle in a new land and have legal ties to the country they came from.
English people formed a **colony** at Jamestown, Virginia, in 1607.

compensate
käm´ pən sāt

v. 1. To make up for, to be equivalent to.
My parents gave me another bike to **compensate** for the one that was stolen.
2. To pay for.
Our student council voted to **compensate** the police officer who spoke to our school about illegal drugs.
compensation *n.* Payment or whatever is given or done to make up for something.
The pedestrian received ten thousand dollars **compensation** for injuries she suffered when struck by the car.

deposit
dē päz´ it

v. 1. To lay down.
The hikers **deposited** their backpacks on the porch.
2. To put money into a bank account or to give as partial payment.
Sign your name on the back before you **deposit** the check.
n. 1. Something laid down.
The flood left a **deposit** of stones on the river banks.
2. Money put into a bank account or given as partial payment.
For a $20 **deposit**, the store will hold the skis.

fascinate
fas´ ə nāt

v. To attract; to strongly hold the interest of.
The circus clowns **fascinated** the children in the audience.
fascinating *adj.* Extremely interesting.
The museum has a **fascinating** display of Native American crafts.

feeble
fē´ bəl

adj. 1. Having little strength, weak.
Lions prey on the most **feeble** zebras in the herd.
2. Not very believable or satisfying.
Henry gave the teacher a **feeble** explanation for being late to class: his watch was broken.

formal
fôr´ məl

adj. 1. Following rules or customs, often in an exact and proper way.
After the summit meeting, the president gave a **formal** dinner at the White House.
2. Suitable for events where strict standards of dress and behavior are expected.
Men's **formal** dress for the evening is white tie and tails.

frigid
frij´ id

adj. 1. Very cold.
The morning air was so **frigid** that Sue's car would not start.
2. Lacking a warm manner; unfriendly.
The **frigid** greeting we received made it clear that we were not welcome.

harsh
härsh

adj. 1. Rough and unpleasant to the senses.
In a **harsh** tone of voice, the farmer ordered us to stay away from the cows.
2. Causing pain; cruel.
Twelve months in jail was a **harsh** sentence for shoplifting.
3. Not suitable for living things; extremely uncomfortable.
Northern Canada's **harsh** climate keeps people from settling there.

huddle
hud´ əl

v. 1. To crowd together.
When the downpour began, we all **huddled** under one umbrella.
2. To curl one's limbs up close to one's body.
During their first night at Mrs. Brisket's school, Bonnie and Sylvia **huddled** under their thin blankets to keep warm.
n. A closely packed group.
The players went into a **huddle** to plan the next play.

remote
rē mōt´

adj. 1. Far away in time or space.
The scientists' route took them through a **remote** region of the Amazon rainforest.
2. Slight or faint.
There was only a **remote** chance of reaching our destination on time.
3. Controlled indirectly or from a distance.
Our garage doors are opened by **remote** control.
4. Distant in manner.
The hotel clerk seemed very **remote** and hardly looked at us when we asked for directions.

resemble
rē zem´ bəl

v. To be like or similar to.
The markings on the wings of the io moth **resemble** the eyes of a small animal and help to protect it.

rigid
rij´ id

adj. 1. Stiff and unbending; not flexible.
The frozen rope was as **rigid** as a stick.
2. Strict; not easily changed.
This school has a **rigid** rule that the police will be informed of any student found with a weapon.

solitary
säl´ ə ter ē

adj. 1. Being alone; lacking the company of others.
In the nineteenth century, lighthouse keepers often led **solitary** lives.
2. Being the only one.
A **solitary** elm grew in the middle of the field.

substantial
səb stan´ shəl

adj. 1. Strong; solid.
The chair is not **substantial** enough to support the weight of an adult.
2. Great in value or size.
I received a **substantial** pay increase after just one year on the job.

waddle
wäd´ əl

v. To walk with short steps, swaying from side to side.
The duck left the pond and **waddled** toward us.
n. An awkward, clumsy walk.
The baby smiled excitedly as he ended his **waddle** across the room.

7A Finding Meanings

Choose two phrases to form a sentence that correctly uses a word from Word List 7. Write each sentence in the space provided.

1. (a) that is operated from a distance.
   (b) that is easy to operate.
   (c) A rigid control is one
   (d) A remote control is one

2. (a) To waddle is to
   (b) To huddle is to
   (c) hold a person's interest or attention.
   (d) curl one's limbs up close to one's body.

3. (a) A deposit is
   (b) A colony is
   (c) a group of creatures living close together.
   (d) a payment given to make up for a loss.

4. (a) To resemble someone
   (b) is to pay that person.
   (c) To compensate someone
   (d) is to apologize to that person.

5. (a) one that goes on too long.
   (b) A formal apology is
   (c) one that is difficult to believe.
   (d) A feeble apology is

6. (a) is not changed easily.
   (b) A rigid attitude is one that
   (c) A frigid attitude is one that
   (d) is no longer practiced.

7. (a) is unpleasantly rough.
   (b) A harsh reply is one that
   (c) is too late to be useful.
   (d) A formal reply is one that

8. (a) A fascinating place is one
   (b) that is in the tropics.
   (c) A frigid place is one
   (d) that is very interesting.

9. (a) that is open to the public.
   (b) A solitary building is one
   (c) A substantial building is one
   (d) that has no others close to it.

10. (a) money given as partial payment.
    (b) A deposit is
    (c) a path that one follows.
    (d) A waddle is

colony

compensate

deposit

fascinate

feeble

formal

frigid

harsh

huddle

remote

resemble

rigid

solitary

substantial

waddle

7B Just the Right Word

Improve each of the following sentences by crossing out the bold phrase and replacing it with a word (or a form of the word) from Word List 7.

1. From a distance crocodiles **look almost the same as** alligators.

2. Sarita's wind-up toy **swayed from side to side as it took short steps** across the floor.

3. A life that is **lived apart from other people** need not be lonely as long as one has books to read.

4. A **very cold** mass of air from Canada caused this wintry weather.

5. The cast on your broken arm will keep it **in a fixed position and prevent it from bending**.

6. The most **strongly built** of the three pigs' houses was the one made of bricks.

7. These patients recovering from operations are so **lacking in strength** that they cannot walk.

8. Meetings with the emperor are very **carefully arranged so as to follow strict rules**.

9. In the **very distant** past all of the continents were joined together.

10. After skiing all day, we **crowded close together** around the fire to get warm.

7C Applying Meanings

Circle the letter of each correct answer to the questions below. A question may have more than one correct answer.

1. Which of the following can be **compensated**?
   (a) an injured person   (c) a person suffering a loss
   (b) a worker   (d) a victim of a crime

2. Which of the following might be **formal**?
   (a) a joke   (c) a request
   (b) a dance   (d) a bow

3. Which of the following might be **substantial**?
   (a) a meal   (c) a sum of money
   (b) the horizon   (d) a purchase

4. Which of the following can be found in **colonies**?
   (a) settlers
   (c) ants
   (b) islands
   (d) mountains

5. Which of the following can be **deposited**?
   (a) money in a bank
   (c) answers on a test
   (b) eggs in a nest
   (d) books on a table

6. Which of the following **resembles** a horse?
   (a) a zebra
   (c) a mule
   (b) a giraffe
   (d) a donkey

7. Which of the following moves with a **waddle**?
   (a) a snake
   (c) a duck
   (b) a frog
   (d) an ostrich

8. Which of the following can be **harsh**?
   (a) a climate
   (c) a voice
   (b) a punishment
   (d) a reward

7D Word Study

Write the antonym of each of the words on the left below in the space next to it. Choose from the words on the right, which are in a different order.

colony
compensate
deposit
fascinate
feeble
formal
frigid
harsh
huddle
remote
resemble
rigid
solitary
substantial
waddle

1. harsh   _____   joy

2. agony   _____   tropical

3. feeble   _____   love

4. escalate   _____   disloyal

5. deposit   _____   flexible

6. rigid   _____   withdraw

7. fascinating   _____   fall

8. frigid   _____   burly

9. steadfast   _____   gentle

10. loathe   _____   boring

Read the passage below; then complete the exercise that follows.

Birds in Tuxedos

What is a bird? A creature that flies, of course. And yet, penguins are birds, but they cannot fly. Their wings are too **feeble** to lift them off the ground. This was not always so. Scientists believe that penguins once flew just like other birds. At some time in the **remote** past, they migrated to Antarctica, the land that surrounds the South Pole. The ice sheet there is two miles thick in places, and the temperature varies between zero in summer and minus seventy degrees in winter. It is possible that penguins were the only creatures that could survive in such a **harsh** climate. Without enemies, they would have no need to use their wings, as other birds do, to escape attacks. Gradually, they would have lost the ability to fly.

Over many thousands of years, the wings of penguins became smaller and more **rigid**. To **compensate** for the loss, it seems, they became excellent swimmers. They use their wings as flippers, while their webbed feet help guide them through the water. They can dive to depths of seventy feet and often leap high out of the water for a breath of air. On land, they **waddle** awkwardly or slide along the ice on their stomachs, but under water they glide gracefully and effortlessly. Penguins spend a lot of time in the sea in a never-ending search for fish, lobsters, crabs, and shrimp, which make up a **substantial** part of their diet.

There are several different kinds of penguins. The smallest is no bigger than a duck, while the largest, called the Emperor penguin, is four feet tall and weighs up to ninety pounds. In addition to the shores of Antarctica, penguins make their homes farther north, on the coasts of South Africa, Australia, and New Zealand, or on the Pacific coast of South America.

Each year for several months, penguins come to land to make nests and lay their eggs. Along the shores of Antarctica, where no plants grow, the penguins gather stones for their nests. Females **deposit** the eggs, chalky white in color and usually no more than two, on the nest. Emperor penguins do not build nests. Instead, after an egg is laid, the male penguin holds it on his feet under a fold of stomach skin, which keeps the egg warm. The female Emperor penguin returns to the **frigid** waters to hunt for food for her family.

For two months, while the baby penguins develop in the eggs, the male Emperor penguins **huddle** close together in **colonies** of up to half a million birds so that they can keep warm. A **solitary** penguin would soon lose its body heat and die in the freezing cold of the long Antarctic night. When the baby penguins break out of the shells, they are unable to see and are quite helpless. For several months they have to be fed by their parents before they are ready to take to the water to find their own food.

On land penguins are unlikely to be mistaken for any other kind of bird. With black feathers covering their backs and snowy white feathers running up their fronts, they **resemble** very short men wearing **formal** dress. Their appearance, combined with the way they walk, makes them look slightly comical. Perhaps this explains in part why we humans find them such **fascinating** creatures.

Answer each of the following questions in the form of a sentence. If a question does not contain a vocabulary word from this lesson's word list, use one in your answer. Use each word only once. Questions and answers will then contain all fifteen words (or forms of the words).

1. Why are penguins a popular feature in aquariums and zoos?

2. What is the meaning of **deposit** as it is used in the passage?

3. In what way do penguins not **resemble** other kinds of birds?

4. What strikes some people as comical about a penguin's appearance?

5. Why did penguins' wings become so **feeble**?

6. How would you describe the summer temperatures of Antarctica?

7. In what way does the passage suggest that penguins were **compensated** for losing the ability to fly?

8. Where do penguins spend much of their time?

9. According to the passage, were penguins ever able to fly?

10. What is the meaning of **rigid** as it is used in the passage?

11. What details in the passage illustrate the **harsh** climate of Antarctica?

12. Why do Emperor penguins gather in large **colonies**?

13. Describe the contrast between the way penguins move on land and in water.

14. What is the meaning of **huddle** as it is used in the passage?

15. What would happen to a penguin that wandered off by itself while on land?

FUN & FASCINATING FACTS

The adjective formed from **colony** is *colonial*. (Virginia was one of the thirteen American *colonies* that declared their independence from British rule in 1776. The town of Williamsburg, Virginia, recreates life in *colonial* America.)

Note that *colony* can also refer to a group of people, especially artists and writers, who come together in a particular place. There they can meet and exchange ideas while working without distractions.

Remote and *distant* are synonyms. Both words mean "far off in distance or time." *Remote,* however, also suggests something cut off and out of the way. Tristan da Cunha, an island in the South Atlantic, and Tokyo, Japan, are each *distant* from New York. But Tokyo is not considered a *remote* city because it is easy to get to by plane. Tristan da Cunha, however, is thought of as a *remote* island because it is difficult to get to.

Solitary is formed from the Latin *solus,* which means "alone." Several other words are formed from the same Latin root. *Solitude* is "the quality or state of being alone." (Henry David Thoreau was seeking *solitude* when he lived alone in the woods near Walden Pond.) *Isolated* means "cut off from the company of others." (We felt *isolated* when the blizzard kept us inside for three days.) *Solitaire* is a card game for just one person.

Lesson 8

> ## Word List
Study the definitions of the words below; then do the exercises for the lesson.

assemble
ə sem´ bəl

v. 1. To bring together into a group; to gather.
At two o'clock we **assembled** at the door of the museum for a tour.
2. To put or fit together.
You need only a screwdriver to **assemble** the bookcase.
assembly *n.* 1. A group of people gathered for a certain purpose.
At the **assembly** this morning, the fire chief will talk to us about fire prevention.
2. The fitting together of various parts.
The **assembly** of the new gas grill took us less than an hour.

banquet
baŋ´ kwət

n. A large meal for many people; a feast.
Six courses were served at the **banquet**, which was given in honor of the teachers who were retiring.

cargo
kär´ go

n. The load carried by a plane or ship.
The **cargo** going to Chile was put into containers and loaded onto the boat.

cask
kask

n. A barrel-shaped container, especially one for holding liquids.
Beverages were imported to colonial New England in large **casks**.

celebrate
sel´ ə brāt

v. To honor something in a special way.
Americans **celebrate** the signing of the Declaration of Independence every Fourth of July.
celebrated *adj.* Famous.
When Charles Dickens toured America, huge crowds turned out to hear the **celebrated** author.

decrease
dē krēs´

v. To become smaller or less.
After June 22, the length of the day gradually **decreases**.
n. The amount by which something becomes smaller.
An outbreak of flu caused a **decrease** in school attendance during January.

desperate
des´ pər ət

adj. 1. Reckless because of feelings of despair.
The action star jumped from a five-story building in a **desperate** attempt to escape her captors.
2. So serious as to be almost hopeless.
The situation of the homeless in our big cities is becoming increasingly **desperate**.

edible
ed´ ə bəl

adj. Safe or fit to be eaten.
Are you certain those mushrooms are **edible**?
n. An item of food; anything that can be eaten.
We'll serve the beverages at this end of the table and the sandwiches and other **edibles** at the other end.

frivolous
friv´ ə ləs

adj. Not serious or important; silly.
Spending money on items like comic books seems **frivolous** to someone who has no money for food.
frivolity *n.* (fri väl´ə tē) Silly or lighthearted play.
The giggling children had to be reminded that **frivolity** has no place at a funeral.

harvest
här´ vəst

n. 1. The gathering of ripe crops for a season.
In Spain, the grape **harvest** begins in late summer.
2. The quantity of crops gathered.
Iowa's corn **harvest** is the largest in years.
v. To gather in the crops.
We usually **harvest** the first peas in April.

hew
hyo͞o

v. 1. To chop down or cut with blows from an ax.
Let's **hew** these dead branches from the tree before they fall and cause damage.
2. To cut or shape with blows of an ax or similar tool.
The Tlingit of the Northwest **hewed** totem poles from tree trunks.

hostile
häs´ təl

adj. Unfriendly; of or like an enemy.
The **hostile** audience would not permit the speaker to finish the speech.
hostility *n.* The expression of unfriendly feelings.
The governor's plan to close the neighborhood school met with so much **hostility** that it was quickly dropped.

pledge
plej

v. To make a serious promise.
A dozen local merchants have **pledged** their support for the new arts program.
n. A serious promise.
Before I was hired, I had to sign a **pledge** that I would not give away company secrets.

prosper
präs´ pər

v. To succeed, especially in terms of money.
Alaska **prospered** when oil was found there.
prosperous *adj.* Enjoying growth and success.
The **prosperous** 1920s ended with the stock market crash of 1929.

task
task

n. A piece of work that needs to be done.
Cutting our way through the underbrush was a difficult **task**.

8A Finding Meanings

Choose two phrases to form a sentence that correctly uses a word from Word List 8. Write each sentence in the space provided.

1. (a) unsure of oneself.
   (b) reckless because of despair.
   (c) To be desperate is to be
   (d) To be prosperous is to be

2. (a) To decrease aid is to
   (b) To pledge aid is to
   (c) abolish it.
   (d) promise it.

3. (a) willingness to make enemies.
   (b) lighthearted play.
   (c) Prosperity is
   (d) Frivolity is

4. (a) To hew something is to   (c) put it together.
   (b) shape it with an ax.   (d) To harvest something is to

5. (a) A celebrated person   (c) is someone who is unfriendly.
   (b) is someone who is careless.   (d) A hostile person

6. (a) A banquet is   (c) a piece of work to be done.
   (b) A task is   (d) payment for work done.

7. (a) A celebrated object   (c) is one that is easily broken.
   (b) An edible object   (d) is one that is famous.

8. (a) is to put it together.   (c) is to shape it by cutting.
   (b) To harvest something   (d) To assemble something

9. (a) A cargo is   (c) the front of a ship.
   (b) A cask is   (d) a barrel used for holding liquids.

10. (a) Banquets are   (c) things that can be eaten.
    (b) seats put around a table.   (d) Edibles are

assemble
banquet
cargo
cask
celebrate
decrease
desperate
edible
frivolous
harvest
hew
hostile
pledge
prosper
task

8B Just the Right Word

Improve each of the following sentences by crossing out the bold phrase and replacing it with a word (or a form of the word) from Word List 8.

1. My cousin thinks television game shows are **silly and lighthearted** and fun to watch.

2. Our fruit stand is **enjoying a great deal of success** this year compared with previous years.

3. My piano teacher says that formal dress is required for the **large dinner at which many people will be served**.

4. Teachers and students **gathered together in a group** outside the building when the alert sounded.

5. The dock workers will unload the **goods carried by the ship** after the passengers go ashore.

6. In August and September all of us worked many hours to help with the **gathering in of the crops**.

7. A count of tourists coming to South Carolina beaches showed a **drop in their number** for the third year in a row.

8. The bright red berries of the yew tree are not **safe to eat**.

9. The situation of those who survived the earthquake was **so serious as to be almost hopeless**.

10. The **unfriendly feelings expressed** at the meeting made me decide to leave early.

8C Applying Meanings

Circle the letter of each correct answer to the questions below. A question may have more than one correct answer.

1. Which of the following might be found in a **cask**?
   (a) pedestrians
   (b) crevices
   (c) water
   (d) potatoes

2. Which of the following might be found at a **banquet**?
   (a) blizzards
   (b) pedestrians
   (c) guests
   (d) beverages

3. Which of the following is a **task**?
   (a) cleaning one's room
   (b) falling asleep
   (c) weeding a garden
   (d) attending college

4. Which of the following can be **assembled**?
   (a) the pieces of a jigsaw puzzle
   (b) the parts of a machine
   (c) a bookcase
   (d) a branch of a tree

5. Which of the following can be **hewed**?
   (a) logs
   (b) trees
   (c) twigs
   (d) paintings

6. Which of the following can be **harvested**?
   (a) apples   (c) mushrooms
   (b) aromas   (d) gales

7. Which of the following do people **celebrate**?
   (a) birthdays   (c) victories
   (b) weddings   (d) retirement

8. Which of the following might be part of a **cargo**?
   (a) grain   (c) oil
   (b) automobiles   (d) nostalgia

8D Word Study

Here are ten Latin words that provide the roots for some English words.

frigus	cold	*aequus*	equal
vivere	to live	*fligere*	to strike
solus	alone	*hostis*	enemy
proximus	nearest	*portare*	to carry
fascinare	to cast a spell on	*desperare*	to give up hope

Fill in the blank spaces in each of the sentences below.

1. A **desperate** person is one who feels trapped in a hopeless situation. The word comes from the Latin _____, meaning _____.

2. To be **solitary** is to be alone. The word comes from the Latin _____, meaning _____.

3. A **hostile** act is one that is unfriendly. The word comes from the Latin _____, meaning _____.

4. If two amounts are **equivalent**, they are equal to each other. The word comes from the Latin _____, meaning _____.

5. An **approximate** number is one that is fairly accurate without being exact. The word comes from the Latin _____, meaning _____,

6. A **frigid** climate is one that is very cold. The word comes from the Latin _____, meaning _____.

assemble
banquet
cargo
cask
celebrate
decrease
desperate
edible
frivolous
harvest
hew
hostile
pledge
prosper
task

7. To **revive** something is to bring it back to life. The word comes from the Latin

_____, meaning _____.

8. To **export** goods is to have them carried to other countries. The word comes from the Latin

_____, meaning _____,.

9. To be absolutely **fascinated** by something is to be spellbound by it. The word comes from

the Latin _____, meaning _____.

10. To **inflict** harm on someone is to hurt that person. The word comes from the Latin

_____, meaning _____.

8E Passage

Read the passage below; then complete the exercise that follows.

The First Thanksgiving

The hundred or so Pilgrims and other passengers who left England in 1620 aboard the *Mayflower* arrived at Plymouth, in what is now Massachusetts. Before going ashore, the forty-one male passengers **assembled** in the ship's main cabin where they wrote the Mayflower Compact. Under this agreement, everyone, Pilgrims and non-Pilgrims alike, would be governed by the same laws. All those present **pledged** to observe the Compact.

Because the Pilgrims came ashore at the end of December, they had to work fast to prepare for winter. Their first **task** was to build shelter to keep themselves safe from animals and bad weather. Soon the sound of axes rang out as trees were chopped down and **hewed** into logs. Next, the *Mayflower's* **cargo** had to be unloaded. There were root vegetables and lemons in crates, sacks of sugar and flour, and cider in **casks**, slabs of salt pork and beef, and seeds for planting in the spring. There were small items of furniture, chests packed with blankets, linens, and clothes. There were family Bibles, tools of all kinds, but no musical instruments—the Pilgrims considered music and dancing to be **frivolous.**

That first winter was a grim one. Food was scarce, and many people became sick and died. By the time the *Mayflower* sailed back to England in the early spring, the number of people remaining had **decreased** to fewer than sixty, and many of these were too feeble to work. Those who had survived the winter were also worried about the Native Americans, who they feared would be **hostile** toward them as new settlers.

One spring day they were very surprised when a Native American walked into their settlement and greeted them in English. His name was Samoset, and he explained that he had learned English from sea captains who had earlier explored the Atlantic coast. He told them of another man, Squanto, who also spoke English. A week or so later he returned with Squanto and sixty Wampanoags, who lived nearby. The colonists were glad that their visitors were friendly for, with their food almost gone, their situation was **desperate**.

Because of the help of these native people, the colonists quickly learned which berries and other fruits were **edible,** where to catch fish, and the best way to grow corn, beans, and squash. When they needed to talk with other native people, Squanto often acted as their translator.

Later in 1621, after the first **harvest**, the colonists held a **banquet** and invited Massasoit, the leader of the Wampanoags, to bring his people to **celebrate** with them. This was the first Thanksgiving; it lasted three days. The worst was now over for the colonists. When the *Mayflower* returned in 1622, it brought more people to join the colony as well as precious supplies. More ships arrived in the following years, and the Plymouth colony grew in size and began to **prosper**. Its future was no longer in doubt.

Answer each of the following questions in the form of a sentence. If a question does not contain a vocabulary word from this lesson's word list, use one in your answer. Use each word only once. Questions and answers will then contain all fifteen words (or forms of the words).

1. What do Americans today do to remember the large dinner that took place at Plymouth in 1621?

2. If the Pilgrims were alive today, what do you suppose they might think of rock concerts?

3. What did the *Mayflower* carry besides the passengers and crew?

4. What **task** did the forty-one male passengers complete before going ashore?

5. What is the meaning of **assembled** as it is used in the passage?

6. What valuable information did the Native Americans give the colonists?

7. What is the meaning of **hewed** as it is used in the passage?

8. Why was it likely that the colonists would obey the rules set out in the Mayflower Compact?

9. What beverage might have been served at the **banquet**?

10. What would happen to the contents of a **cask** if it got a hole in it?

11. What might the colonists have **harvested** in 1621?

12. In what way did the Native Americans surprise the colonists?

13. How many colonists survived the first winter?

14. Why might the survivors of the first winter have felt **desperate**?

15. How do you think life in the colony changed as it **prospered**?

FUN & FASCINATING FACTS

The antonym of **edible** is *inedible*. (The food was so overcooked that it was *inedible*.) Another antonym is *poisonous*. (Cultivated mushrooms are *edible*, but some wild mushrooms are *poisonous*.)

Don't confuse **hew** with *hue*, which is a color or shade of color. (Aqua is a blue color with a greenish *hue*.) These two words are homophones; they are pronounced the same, but have different meanings and spellings.

Pledge and *promise* are synonyms, but a pledge is a serious promise, made concerning something important. You might *promise* to meet a friend after school; you *pledge* allegiance to the flag of the United States and to the republic for which it stands.

Review for Lessons 5–8

Crossword Puzzle Solve the crossword puzzle below by studying the clues and filling in the answer boxes. Clues followed by a number are definitions of words in Lessons 5 through 8. The number gives the lesson from which the answer to the clue is taken.

Clues Across

1. The highest part (5)
6. To become less or fewer (8)
7. Opposite of strong
9. Lacking strength (7)
10. The largest city in Nebraska
14. To put into a different language (6)
15. Short for "New York City"
18. A cheerful, hopeful person (5)
21. To hate or despise (6)
22. The way to get to a place (5)
23. To promise (8)
24. Safe to eat (8)
25. To gather in crops (8)

Clues Down

2. Used as a temporary replacement (5)
3. To cause to bear something painful (6)
4. Unpleasant; disturbing (6)
5. To chop or cut down with an ax (8)
8. Great pain and suffering (6)
11. Unfriendly (8)
12. Very wicked; terrible (6)
13. To succeed; to do well (8)
16. A deep narrow opening (5)
17. To walk with an awkward, swaying movement (7)
19. A large country in Asia
20. To tempt with a promise of something (5)

Lesson 9

Word List
Study the definitions of the words below; then do the exercises for the lesson.

absurd
ab sʉrd´

adj. So unreasonable as to be laughable; foolish or silly.
You'd look **absurd** in a suit and tie at the beach.

accomplish
ə käm´ plish

v. To do something by making an effort; to complete successfully.
I know I will **accomplish** these errands by noon.
accomplishment *n.* Something requiring skill and determination that is completed successfully.
Anne Sullivan's great **accomplishment** was to teach a deaf and blind child to speak and to read.

ascend
ə send´

v. To rise, usually in a steady way.
The rocket **ascended** to a height of five hundred feet before falling to earth.

dense
dens

adj. 1. Tightly packed; crowded close together.
The tired explorers hacked their way through **dense** vines and bushes to reach the coast.
2. Thick; hard to see through.
At the airport there was such **dense** fog that planes couldn't take off.
3. Stupid, thickheaded.
I don't want to seem **dense**, but I don't understand your question.

experiment
ek sper´ ə mənt

n. A test to prove or discover something.
The **experiment** shows that oxygen and hydrogen combine to form water.
v. 1. To carry out experiments.
Benjamin Franklin **experimented** with a kite to show that lightning was a form of electricity.
2. To try out new ideas or activities.
A good cook **experiments** with different herbs and spices to create new dishes.

flimsy
flim´ zē

adj. 1. Easily damaged or broken; not strongly made.
The cart was too **flimsy** to carry such a heavy load.
2. Not believable.
Saying you lost your pen is a **flimsy** excuse for not doing your homework.

heroic
hi rō´ ik

adj. 1. Very brave; showing great courage.
The teenager dove into the pond and made a **heroic** rescue of the child who couldn't swim.
2. Showing great determination; requiring enormous effort.
Firefighters made a **heroic** effort to put out the blaze.

lumber
lum´ bər

n. Wood that has been sawed into boards.
Have you ordered the **lumber** for the deck you are building?
v. To move in a clumsy or heavy way.
The fat old dog **lumbered** toward me.

mimic
mim´ ik

v. 1. To copy or imitate closely.
The parrot fascinated us because it could **mimic** human speech so well.
2. To make fun of by imitating.
I got upset when you **mimicked** my friend's limp.
n. One who can imitate sounds, speech, or actions.
A good **mimic** carefully studies the person being imitated.

significant sig nif´ ə kənt	*adj.* Important; full of meaning. July 4, 1776, is a **significant** date in American history. **significance** *n.* The quality of being important or of giving meaning. The **significance** of the Bill of Rights is that it spells out important freedoms enjoyed by all Americans.
soar sôr	*v.* 1. To fly high in the sky. We watched the eagles **soar** until they were just specks in the sky. 2. To rise suddenly and rapidly. The cost of a college education is expected to **soar** during the next few years.
spectator spek´ tāt ər	*n.* A person who watches an activity; an onlooker. The **spectators** jostled each other as they rushed onto the field at the end of the game.
suspend sə spend´	*v.* 1. To hang while attached to something above. The hammock was **suspended** from the porch ceiling. 2. To stop for a while before going on. The inspector **suspended** work on the building until the contractor obtained the proper permits. 3. To bar from working, attending, or taking part for a while. The students caught cheating were **suspended** from school for one week.
terminate tʉr´ mə nāt	*v.* To bring or to come to an end. Heavy rain **terminated** the tennis match after only ten minutes of play.
unwieldy un wēl´ dē	*adj.* Hard to handle or control because of large size or heaviness. The sofa was so **unwieldy** that getting it up three flights of stairs was a real challenge.

9A Finding Meanings

Choose two phrases to form a sentence that correctly uses a word from Word List 9. Write each sentence in the space provided.

absurd
accomplish
ascend
dense
experiment
flimsy
heroic
lumber
mimic
significant
soar
spectator
suspend
terminate
unwieldy

1. (a) If you suspend something,
   (b) you make a copy of it.
   (c) you bring it to an end.
   (d) If you terminate something,

2. (a) is easily broken.
   (b) is tightly packed.
   (c) Something that is dense
   (d) Something that is unwieldy

3. (a) To accomplish something
   (b) is to complete it successfully.
   (c) is to raise it to a higher level.
   (d) To mimic something

4. (a) that ends quickly.
   (b) A heroic effort is one
   (c) that shows great determination.
   (d) An absurd effort is one

5. (a) To ascend is to   (c) test or try out an idea.
   (b) To experiment is to   (d) increase in size or amount.

6. (a) A flimsy container is one that   (c) is not strongly made.
   (b) An unwieldy container is one that   (d) is meant to hold liquids.

7. (a) go to a higher level.   (c) fall into a drowsy state.
   (b) To ascend is to   (d) To lumber is to

8. (a) someone who hears.   (c) A spectator is
   (b) someone who watches.   (d) A mimic is

9. (a) move in a clumsy way.   (c) To soar is to
   (b) To lumber is to   (d) feel pain or discomfort.

10. (a) that is meaningful.   (c) An absurd statement is one
    (b) A significant statement is one   (d) that goes on longer than necessary.

9B Just the Right Word

Improve each of the following sentences by crossing out the bold phrase and replacing it with a word (or a form of the word) from Word List 9.

1. The movie is about the **very brave** women and men who fight forest fires.

2. The bicyclists could not see through the **very thick** fog.

3. The comedian usually gets lots of laughs when he **imitates the sound of** the voices of famous movie stars.

4. Francine's story about seeing a live dinosaur is **too silly to be believed**.

5. The *Mayflower* passengers' spirits **suddenly rose** when they got their first sight of land.

6. Leave the box where it is if you think it is too **large to be picked up and carried easily**.

7. Coach Louis told us that any player who fails a course is **not allowed to take part in any games** for the rest of the season.

8. My family's visit to the Vietnam Veterans Memorial in Washington, D.C., was especially **full of meaning** because my uncle's name appears there.

9. Ms. Smith's **carefully controlled attempt to discover if it was possible** to grow orchids indoors year-round was very successful.

10. The **wood that has been sawed into boards** is stacked outside so that it will dry.

9C Applying Meanings

Circle the letter of each correct answer to the questions below. A question may have more than one correct answer.

1. Which of the following can be **dense**?
   (a) a person
   (b) a crowd
   (c) a hole
   (d) a forest

2. Which of the following can **soar**?
   (a) hopes
   (b) cows
   (c) prices
   (d) birds

3. Which of the following would be an **accomplishment**?
   (a) going to jail
   (b) winning a gold medal
   (c) cheating on a test
   (d) eating a pizza

4. Which of the following can be **suspended**?
   (a) a bird feeder
   (b) a mistake
   (c) work
   (d) a student

5. Which of the following would be **unwieldy**?
   (a) a piano
   (b) a flute
   (c) a 36-inch television set
   (d) a sleep sofa

6. Which of the following could have **significance**?
   (a) a marriage
   (b) a death
   (c) a graduation
   (d) a birth

7. Which of the following might you **experiment** with?
   (a) hair styles
   (b) a chemistry set
   (c) clothing
   (d) food

absurd
accomplish
ascend
dense
experiment
flimsy
heroic
lumber
mimic
significant
soar
spectator
suspend
terminate
unwieldy

8. Which of the following can be **flimsy**?

    (a) an aroma   (c) a shelter

    (b) a task   (d) an excuse

9D Word Study

Words that have different meanings and different spellings but sound the same are called homophones. Here are five pairs of homophones:

prey/pray   course/coarse   route/root   hew/hue   soar/sore

Look at each of the sentences below and decide whether the word in bold is being used correctly. Put a check mark next to each correct use and an X next to each incorrect use.

1. We tried to get to the **route** of the problem. _____

2. The wolf seized its **prey** in its jaws. _____

3. I will **prey** for the safe return of those still missing. _____

4. The coastal **root** is the quickest way into town. _____

5. Nigel's manners are rather **course**. _____

6. We watched the rocket **soar** until it was out of sight. _____

7. Muslims **pray** to Allah. _____

8. A **soar** knee kept me from taking part in the race. _____

9. We left the harbor and set a **coarse** for Nantucket. _____

10. The **route** to the mountain summit is well marked. _____

11. Sharp tools were needed to **hew** the boat from a single log. _____

12. My job was to **hue** the branches from the tree. _____

13. The cost of living is expected to **sore** in the coming year. _____

14. **Coarse** salt is made up of larger grains. _____

15. The daffodils were a deep yellow **hue**. _____

9E Passage

Read the passage below; then complete the exercise that follows.

The Sky's the Limit

For as long as people have watched birds **soar** far above the earth, they have dreamed of being able to fly. The Montgolfier brothers of France, Jacques and Joseph, thought of a way this might be possible. In 1782, after observing smoke and hot air rising from a fire, they made a small cloth balloon, filled it with hot air, and watched it rise seventy feet. Hot air is less **dense** than cold air and so is lighter. The warmer, lighter air inside the balloon caused it to rise.

The next year they built a balloon with a diameter of thirty-five feet. They filled it with hot air by burning wool and straw on an iron grate that rested in a large basket **suspended** beneath the balloon. After this rose successfully, they built another one, which was even bigger. In September 1783, before a large crowd, which included the French royal family, the Montgolfier brothers placed a sheep, a duck, and a rooster in the balloon's basket and released it. The balloon **ascended** to a height of fifteen hundred feet and stayed in the air for eight minutes.

A hot-air balloon rises because it is lighter than the air around it, but the idea that something heavier than air could ever get off the ground seemed **absurd** to most people. Not everyone thought so, however. By the late 1800s, after the invention of the steam engine and, later on, the much lighter gasoline engine, the first airplanes were being made. Some of these had movable wings to **mimic** the flapping of birds' wings, but they were too **unwieldy** to fly. Some were powered by steam engines, which made them so heavy they couldn't get off the ground. But when the airplane's frame was made lighter, the plane became **flimsy**. Because of this problem, many early flights **terminated** in a crash. Some people believed that to fly in those days was almost a **heroic** act.

It took another pair of brothers, Orville and Wilbur Wright, to figure out how to build a machine that could stay up in the air. The Wright brothers made and repaired bicycles for a living at their shop in Dayton, Ohio. Like many other people at the time, the idea of flying fascinated them. After **experimenting** with kites and gliders, they built a plane with rigid wings that was powered by a small gasoline engine. This was much lighter than a steam engine.

December 17, 1903, is a **significant** date in the history of flying. On that day at Kitty Hawk, North Carolina, the Wright brothers demonstrated that a heavier-than-air machine could successfully fly. Just a handful of **spectators** watched as the plane, with Orville Wright at the controls, began to **lumber** across the grassy field. They cheered as they saw the plane lift off the ground and stay in the air for twelve seconds before landing about 120 feet away.

That afternoon the Wright brothers made three more flights—the longest, lasting fifty-nine seconds, covered 852 feet. They had **accomplished** their goal and made it possible for humans to fulfill their dreams of flight. One hundred years later, an exact copy of the Wright brothers' plane was built. To celebrate the one hundredth birthday of their achievement, it was supposed to make a flight at Kitty Hawk on December 17, 2003. It looked just like the Wright Brothers' plane, but sadly it failed to get off the ground. You can see the airplane the Wright brothers built at the National Air and Space Museum in Washington, D.C.

absurd
accomplish
ascend
dense
experiment
flimsy
heroic
lumber
mimic
significant
soar
spectator
suspend
terminate
unwieldy

Answer each of the following questions in the form of a sentence. If a question does not contain a vocabulary word from this lesson's word list, use one in your answer. Use each word only once. Questions and answers will then contain all fifteen words (or forms of the words).

1. Why is a hot-air balloon able to rise?

2. Why is Kitty Hawk, North Carolina, **significant** in the history of flying?

3. Describe one **accomplishment** of the Montgolfier brothers.

4. How high did the first balloon of the Montgolfier brothers rise?

5. Why were the early airplanes with flapping wings unsuccessful?

6. What is the meaning of **soar** as it is used in the passage?

7. What important family saw the Montgolfiers' hot-air balloon in September 1783?

8. What is the meaning of **suspended** as it is used in the passage?

9. Why were injuries a common occurrence among the first fliers?

10. Why did some early planes have movable wings?

11. How did the Wright brothers test their ideas before building the first airplane?

12. What is the meaning of **lumber** as it is used in the passage?

13. What problem developed when airplane frames were made lighter?

14. What might an aircraft designer of today think of the idea of using a steam engine to power an airplane?

15. Why is it not considered **heroic** to fly in today's airplanes?

FUN & FASCINATING FACTS

The noun formed from **ascend** is *ascent,* the act of rising or going higher. (Our *ascent* to the summit took approximately four hours.) The antonyms of these words are *descend* and *descent*. Don't confuse *ascent* with its homophone *assent*. *Assent* means "agreement." (We cannot give our *assent* to the new proposal until the changes we asked for are made.)

Soar and *sore* are also homophones. A *sore* is a painful spot on the body, often with the skin broken. *Sore* is also an *adjective* and means "painful."

Spectator is formed from the Latin *spectare,* which means "to see" or "to look at." Two other words formed from this root are *inspect* and *spectacles*. When you inspect something, you *look at* it closely; *spectacles,* another word for eyeglasses, help a person to *see* better.

A *pendant* is something that hangs from a chain around a person's neck. This word comes from the Latin *pendere,* which means "to hang." **Suspend** comes from the same Latin root.

The Latin *terminus* means "end." It provides the root for the verb **terminate**. Several other words are formed from this root. A *terminus* is the end of a bus or train line. *Terminal* means "of or relating to an end." A *terminal* illness is one that ends in death. Something that is *interminable* seems to go on without an end. (After an *interminable* wait, we finally saw the doctor.)

Lesson 10

Word List
Study the definitions of the words below; then do the exercises for the lesson.

available
ə vāl´ ə bəl

adj. Easy to get; present and ready for use.
The salesperson said the jacket was **available** in black, brown, and white.

bondage
bän´ dij

n. The state of being a slave.
More than **three** thousand years ago, Moses led the Jewish people out of **bondage** in Egypt.

donate
dō´ nāt

v. To give to those in need, often through an organization.
People across the country **donated** food and clothing to the victims of the flood.
donation *n.* Whatever is donated, as money or goods.
Donations to help rebuild the community center now total sixty thousand dollars.

establish
e stab´ lish

v. 1. To set up or begin.
Established in 1636, Harvard College, now part of Harvard University, is the oldest college in the United States.
2. To show to be true.
Scientists have **established** beyond any doubt that smoking causes cancer and other diseases.
establishment *n.* Something that has been established, especially a place of business or a public building.
Many restaurants, stores, and other **establishments** now ban smoking.

evade
ē vād´

v. 1. To keep away from; to avoid being caught.
The chipmunk **evaded** the cat by scrambling up a tree.
2. To avoid doing or answering.
Persons who **evade** paying income taxes can find themselves in serious trouble.
evasive *adj.* Carefully avoiding saying too much; not open or direct.
The captured prisoners were **evasive** when asked who had helped them escape.

liberate
lib´ ər āt

v. To free.
A group objecting to experiments on animals opened the monkey cages and **liberated** the animals inside them.

numerous
nōō´ mər əs

adj. A large number; very many.
The bus makes **numerous** stops before it leaves us at school.

occasion
ō kā´ zhən

n. 1. A particular time.
I recognized Marcia at once because we had met on a previous **occasion**.
2. A special event.
The presentation in Oslo, Norway, of the 1992 Nobel Peace Prize to Rigoberta Menchu was a great **occasion** for the Guatemalan people.
occasional *adj.* Happening once in a while.
We make an **occasional** trip to town to pick up supplies.

oppose
ə pōz´

v. To be or act against.
Moin, my best friend, will **oppose** me in the tennis finals.
opposition *n.* (äp ə zish´ ən) The act or condition of being against.
There was no **opposition** to the proposal, which passed by a vote of 16 to 0.

prohibit prō hib´ it	*v.* To forbid by law or order. The law now **prohibits** smoking in many public places.
pursue pər soō´	*v.* 1. To follow in order to capture; to chase. Police **pursued** the stolen car in a high-speed chase across town. 2. To seek actively; to carry on with. Do you intend to **pursue** a career in medicine? **pursuit** *n.* 1. The act of following after. In the early 1930s, people desperate for work poured into cities in **pursuit** of jobs. 2. An activity, as a job or sport, that a person takes part in. Jennie and Bruce enjoy canoeing and other outdoor **pursuits** during the summer.
reassure rē ə shoor´	*v.* To make less worried or fearful; to comfort. I was nervous before the recital, but my piano teacher **reassured** me. **reassurance** *n.* The act of giving comfort or the state of receiving comfort. Coach Ward's **reassurances** made us more optimistic about our chances of winning.
reluctant rē luk´ tənt	*adj.* Not wanting to do something; unwilling. We were **reluctant** to leave our warm beds when we saw the ice on the windows. **reluctance** *n.* The state of not wanting to do something. With great **reluctance**, I agreed to clean my room before my cousins arrived on Saturday.
superior sə pir´ ē ər	*adj.* 1. Excellent of its kind. Margot made the team because she is a **superior** runner. 2. Higher in position or rank. A cardinal is **superior** to a bishop in the Catholic church. *n.* A person of higher rank. I reported to my **superior** as soon as I returned to work.
yearn yʉrn	*v.* To want very badly; to be filled with longing. Dorothy told the Wizard of Oz that she **yearned** to be back in Kansas. **yearning** *n.* A longing or strong desire. As rain leaked slowly through the roof of our tent, I was filled with a **yearning** for my warm, dry bed at home.

available
bondage
donate
establish
evade
liberate
numerous
occasion
oppose
prohibit
pursue
reassure
reluctant
superior
yearn

10A Finding Meanings

Choose two phrases to form a sentence that correctly uses a word from Word List 10. Write each sentence in the space provided.

1. (a) a promise to do certain things.
   (b) An establishment is
   (c) a place of business.
   (d) A yearning is

2. (a) have important people calling.
   (b) have many people calling.
   (c) To have numerous visitors is to
   (d) To have occasional visitors is to

3. (a) To liberate someone is to
   (b) To pursue someone is to
   (c) chase that person.
   (d) put that person in prison.

4. (a) To remember an occasion is to
   (b) recall a particular person.
   (c) To remember a donation is to
   (d) recall a particular time.

5. (a) a deep longing.
   (b) A superior is
   (c) someone younger than oneself.
   (d) A yearning is

6. (a) To reassure someone is to
   (b) meet that person again.
   (c) put that person's mind at ease.
   (d) To oppose someone is to

7. (a) To be superior is
   (b) to act in a foolhardy way.
   (c) To be reluctant is
   (d) to be better than average.

8. (a) avoid answering them.
   (b) To prohibit questions is to
   (c) ask them over and over.
   (d) To evade questions is to

9. (a) Liberation is
   (b) an unwillingness to act.
   (c) a state of slavery.
   (d) Bondage is

10. (a) be against it.
    (b) set it free.
    (c) To donate something is to
    (d) To oppose something is to

10B Just the Right Word

Improve each of the following sentences by crossing out the bold phrase and replacing it with a word (or a form of the word) from Word List 10.

1. We managed to **get away from** the hornets by running into the house.

2. Tickets for this Saturday's concert are **easy to obtain** from most music stores.

3. The manager was **not very willing** to return my deposit when I cancelled my order for the ski boots.

4. I have to check with a **person of a higher rank** before I can let you in the building on Saturday.

5. My **going in search** of information about lasers led me to spend a lot of time in the library.

6. It has been **shown to be true** that the sun is about five billion years old.

7. Wintergreen Junior High School is seeking **gifts of money** to pay for the sports program.

8. What **special event** are you celebrating with this beautiful cake?

9. The city **does not allow** downtown parking for the duration of the street festival.

10. Paris was **freed from the foreign army that occupied it** on August 25, 1944.

10C Applying Meanings

Circle the letter of each correct answer to the questions below. A question may have more than one correct answer.

1. Which of the following might a person **pursue**?
   - (a) an education
   - (b) a runaway horse
   - (c) an illness
   - (d) a career

2. Which of the following might a person **yearn** for?
   - (a) freedom
   - (b) agony
   - (c) despair
   - (d) prosperity

3. Which of the following statements offers **reassurance**?
   - (a) "It'll be okay."
   - (b) "You can do it."
   - (c) "You'll be sorry."
   - (d) "Don't say I didn't warn you."

4. Which of the following statements shows **reluctance**?
   - (a) "Let's go."
   - (b) "I'll have to think about it."
   - (c) "What's the hurry?"
   - (d) "Let's not be too hasty."

5. Which of the following do you **oppose**?
   - (a) careless driving
   - (b) vacations
   - (c) education
   - (d) crime

available
bondage
donate
establish
evade
liberate
numerous
occasion
oppose
prohibit
pursue
reassure
reluctant
superior
yearn

6. Which of the following could be **established**?

(a) a fact

(c) a restaurant

(b) a hospital

(d) a colony

7. Which of the following could be **evasive**?

(a) a reply

(c) an explanation

(b) a house

(d) a demand

8. Which of the following might a person **donate**?

(a) space

(c) time

(b) money

(d) food

10D Word Study

Look at each group of four words below. If you think two of the words in a group are synonyms, circle those words and write *S* in the space next to the words.

If you think two of the words in a group are antonyms, circle those words and write *A* in the space next to the words.

1. yearn	ascend	rise	lumber	_____
2. decrease	prosper	end	terminate	_____
3. oppose	deposit	support	return	_____
4. lessen	decrease	suspend	donate	_____
5. donate	receive	retire	translate	_____
6. flimsy	wicked	sturdy	nostalgic	_____
7. capture	prohibit	liberate	remove	_____
8. yearning	desire	concept	bondage	_____
9. return	reassure	abolish	establish	_____
10. willing	alert	puny	reluctant	_____

Read the passage below; then complete the exercise that follows.

With Moses to the Promised Land

Harriet Tubman was born a slave in Maryland in 1820, but from the time she was a young child, she **yearned** to be free. The hard physical work that she was forced to do made her very strong, and although as a slave she received no education, she was also intelligent and quick-thinking. She put these qualities to good use, first in making her own escape and later in helping others to do the same.

When Harriet was in her late twenties, her owner died. Fearing she would be sold and sent to the deep South, where the work was harder and slave owners more cruel, she decided to escape. She urged her brothers to come with her on the journey north, and they **reluctantly** joined her. Soon after they set out, afraid of being caught, they turned back. So Harriet continued alone, traveling mostly at night, and made it safely to Philadelphia. Although she had found freedom, she couldn't enjoy it because so many others, including her family, were still living in **bondage**.

In 1850, Congress passed a law making it a crime to help runaway slaves. But over the next eleven years, Harriet returned **numerous** times to the South to lead other slaves to Canada, where slavery was **prohibited** and escaped slaves were welcome. Altogether during this time she helped to **liberate** over three hundred people, including her parents and brothers and sisters. Along the way she stayed with people who offered food and shelter in their homes, often at great risk to themselves. These houses were called "stations" on what became known as the Underground Railroad.

Between trips, Harriet took whatever jobs were **available**—cooking, sewing, or cleaning. She used some of her money to help former slaves start new lives and saved some of it for her next journey south. She had many friends who **opposed** slavery; when she needed money for her work, they would help her by making **donations**.

Slave owners, furious at having their "property" stolen, offered as much as $40,000 for Harriet Tubman's capture. She was often **pursued** by people who wanted the reward. She had many narrow escapes, but she always managed to **evade** being caught. Escaping slaves called her Moses because she led them to freedom, just as Moses had led the Jewish people out of slavery in Egypt thousands of years earlier.

During the Civil War, Harriet Tubman worked for the North as a nurse in the Union army. Slaves had been taught by their owners to be afraid of the Union soldiers, but Harriet went behind enemy lines and was able to **reassure** them. They believed her when she told them they had nothing to fear from the Union army. On some **occasions** while there, she acted as a spy, reporting to her **superiors** when she returned to the Union side. After the war she worked energetically to start schools in the South for the freed slaves, even though she herself could not read or write. She eventually settled in Auburn, New York, where she **established** a nursing home for elderly African Americans. When she died in 1913, thousands mourned this courageous woman who had helped so many people.

available
bondage
donate
establish
evade
liberate
numerous
occasion
oppose
prohibit
pursue
reassure
reluctant
superior
yearn

Answer each of the following questions in the form of a sentence. If a question does not contain a vocabulary word from this lesson's word list, use one in your answer. Use each word only once. Questions and answers will then contain all fifteen words (or forms of the words).

1. What did the law that Congress passed in 1850 **prohibit**?

2. What is the meaning of the word **superiors** as it is used in the passage?

3. How did Harriet Tubman feel about being a slave?

4. Why were her brothers **reluctant** to go with Tubman?

5. How did Harriet Tubman's friends help her?

6. What is the meaning of **evade** as it is used in the passage?

7. Why was Harriet Tubman called Moses by those she helped?

8. How do you think Tubman might have **reassured** the slaves she was helping?

9. In what way did the stations on the Underground Railroad help to **liberate** the slaves?

10. Why do you think some people opened their homes to escaping slaves?

11. How did the reward for her capture affect Tubman's later trips to the South?

12. What is the meaning of **established** as it is used in the passage?

13. Why do you think most slaves were unable to read or write?

14. What two activities did Tubman engage in during the Civil War?

15. Why do you think Tubman made **numerous** trips south even though it was very dangerous for her?

FUN & FASCINATING FACTS

The Statue of *Liberty* is a symbol of freedom to people all over the world. To hand out money *liberally* is to hand it out freely, without exercising very much control. Both these words, together with **liberate**, are formed from the Latin *liber*, which means "free." It's interesting to note that the Latin word for "book" is also *liber*. (A *library* is a place where *books* are kept.) There is a clear connection between books and freedom. A person who cannot read a book is in a kind of prison; learning to read sets the mind free to explore the world and everything in it.

The noun formed from the verb **prohibit** is *prohibition*, an order to stop or the act of forbidding. The word is associated with a fascinating period in United States history. In 1919, the Eighteenth Amendment to the Constitution prohibited the sale of alcoholic beverages. The result was that many citizens ignored the law, and gangsters such as Al Capone grew rich by illegally selling alcoholic beverages. Within a few years it was clear that the amendment had failed. Prohibition, as this time was known, ended in 1933 when the Twenty-first Amendment was added to the Constitution. This one abolished the Eighteenth.

Lesson 11

Word List

Study the definitions of the words below; then do the exercises for the lesson.

accelerate
ak sel´ ər āt

v. 1. To go or to cause to go faster.
The morning train quickly **accelerates** once it leaves the station.
2. To bring about at an earlier time.
Increased sunlight **accelerates** the growth of plants.

altitude
al´ tə tōōd

n. Height above sea level or the earth's surface.
Mexico City lies at an **altitude** of almost 8,000 feet.

anxious
aŋk´ shəs

adj. 1. Worried; concerned.
I am **anxious** about how I did on the Spanish test.
2. Eager; wishing strongly.
After writing to each other for over a year, the two penpals are **anxious** to meet.
anxiety *n.* (aŋ zī´ ə tē) Great uneasiness or concern.
Our **anxiety** increased as road conditions got steadily worse.

brace
brās

v. 1. To make stronger by giving support to.
Mom **braced** the table leg with a metal strip to keep it from wobbling.
2. To make ready for a shock; to prepare.
After the pilot's warning, we **braced** ourselves for a bumpy landing.
n. Something used to support a weak part.
I wore a **brace** on my leg for four weeks after I injured it doing a high jump.
bracing *adj.* Giving energy to; refreshing.
After spending most of the summer in the city, we found the mountain air wonderfully **bracing**.

confident
kän´ fi dant

adj. Certain; sure.
We are **confident** we will win Saturday's hockey game.
confidence *n.* 1. A lack of doubt; a feeling of being certain.
My parents showed their **confidence** in me by letting me repair the car by myself.
2. Trust in another to keep a secret.
Because Felix told me this in **confidence**, I cannot answer your question.

contact
kän´ takt

n. 1. The touching or joining of two things.
Contact with a live wire will give you an electric shock.
2. The condition of being in communication with others.
Before the telephone was invented, people usually stayed in **contact** by writing letters.
v. To communicate with.
The Apollo astronauts could not **contact** Earth while their spaceship was traveling behind the moon.

exult
eg zult´

v. To be joyful; to show great happiness.
Senator Gray's supporters **exulted** when she easily won reelection.
exultant *adj.* Very happy.
Theresa was **exultant** when she crossed the 10K finish line first.

hangar
haŋ´ ər

n. A building where aircraft are kept and repaired.
The pilot steered the plane out of the **hangar** and onto the runway.

83

maximum
maks´ i məm

n. The greatest or highest number or amount.
The largest bus we have for school trips holds a **maximum** of fifty people.
adj. Being the greatest or highest number or amount.
The **maximum** speed of this car is 150 miles per hour.

methodical
mə thäd´ i kəl

adj. Done in a regular, orderly way.
Our **methodical** search of the house failed to turn up any evidence of a robbery.

nonchalant
nän shə länt´

adj. Having the appearance of not caring; seeming to show a lack of concern.
Your **nonchalant** attitude to schoolwork worries your parents.

proceed
prō sēd´

v. To go on, especially after stopping for a while; to continue.
The subway train **proceeded** on its way after I got off at 14th Street.

saunter
sôn´ tər

v. To walk without hurrying; to stroll in a relaxed, unhurried manner.
Pedestrians **saunter** along the river bank, enjoying the afternoon sunshine.
n. A relaxed, unhurried walk.
Our **saunter** around the park was abruptly terminated by a violent thunderstorm.

solo
sō´ lō

n. A musical piece for one voice or a single instrument.
A jubilant violin **solo** begins the symphony's second movement.
adj. Made or done by one person.
Francis Chichester's **solo** voyage around the world made him famous.
v. To fly alone, especially for the first time.
Most student pilots **solo** after ten hours of lessons.

stall
stôl

n. 1. A place for an animal in a barn.
Each cow in the barn had its own **stall**.
2. A small stand or booth where things are sold.
I purchased this pottery at one of the **stalls** at the county fair.
v. 1. To suddenly lose power.
You will **stall** the engine if you let out the clutch too quickly.
2. To delay by being evasive.
Tenants sometimes try to **stall** the landlord when they can't pay the rent.

accelerate
altitude
anxious
brace
confident
contact
exult
hangar
maximum
methodical
nonchalant
proceed
saunter
solo
stall

11A Finding Meanings

Choose two phrases to form a sentence that correctly uses a word from Word List 11. Write each sentence in the space provided.

1. (a) A plane's hangar is
   (b) the amount of cargo it can carry.
   (c) its height above sea level.
   (d) A plane's altitude is

2. (a) To accelerate an engine is to
   (b) cause it to lose power suddenly.
   (c) run it at its lowest speed.
   (d) To stall an engine is to

3. (a) a performance by one person.   (c) A solo is
   (b) A saunter is   (d) a support for a broken part.

4. (a) a place where goods are sold.   (c) A brace is
   (b) a place where planes are kept.   (d) A hangar is

5. (a) stop suddenly.   (c) go faster.
   (b) To accelerate is to   (d) To exult is to

6. (a) does things in an orderly way.   (c) An anxious person
   (b) is filled with happiness.   (d) A methodical person

7. (a) A contact is   (c) a support for a broken part.
   (b) A brace is   (d) a place where business is done.

8. (a) To be nonchalant about something is   (c) to be concerned about it.
   (b) To be anxious about something is   (d) to be very happy about it.

9. (a) To be confident is to be   (c) reluctant to act or speak.
   (b) sure of oneself.   (d) To be exultant is to be

10. (a) walk in a relaxed, unhurried manner. (c) To saunter is to
    (b) show a willingness to help.   (d) To proceed is to

11B Just the Right Word

Improve each of the following sentences by crossing out the bold phrase and replacing it with a word (or a form of the word) from Word List 11.

1. Five striped bass is the **greatest number** you are allowed to catch this month.

2. After checking our coats, we will **make our way** to our seats in the upper balcony.

3. Canadian baseball fans were **filled with happiness** when the Blue Jays won the World Series.

4. I plan to **fly a plane without my instructor** tomorrow.

5. The breeze off the ocean is very **refreshing and gives one renewed energy**.

6. The trainer led the horse back to its **enclosed place in the stable** after her ride.

7. I lost **the possibility to communicate** with my friends after they moved out of state.

8. The skiers were **showing no concern** as they started down the steep slope.

9. Jan was up at dawn, **very eager** to be on his way.

10. I am telling you what the lawyer told me in **the expectation that you will keep it a secret**.

11C Applying Meanings

Circle the letter of each correct answer to the questions below. A question may have more than one correct answer.

1. Which of the following are measurements of **altitude**?
   - (a) three tons
   - (b) twenty dollars
   - (c) six miles
   - (d) 10,000 feet

2. Which of the following might you find in a **hangar**?
   - (a) airplanes
   - (b) spare parts
   - (c) tools
   - (d) horses

3. Which of the following might cause a person to **exult**?
   - (a) receiving a scholarship
   - (b) being liberated
   - (c) an exceptional harvest
   - (d) being thrown into bondage

4. Which of the following remarks shows **confidence**?
   - (a) "I give up."
   - (b) "I can do it."
   - (c) "I'm not sure."
   - (d) "Let me show you how."

5. Which of the following can be **accelerated**?
   - (a) plant growth
   - (b) an automobile
   - (c) a route
   - (d) a crevice

accelerate

altitude

anxious

brace

confident

contact

exult

hangar

maximum

methodical

nonchalant

proceed

saunter

solo

stall

6. Which of the following might cause **anxiety**?

   (a) becoming ill   (c) being denounced

   (b) losing a job   (d) finding a wallet

7. Which of the following can **stall**?

   (a) a horse   (c) an airplane

   (b) an engine   (d) a person

8. Which of the following could be used as a **brace**?

   (a) a steel rod   (c) a length of string

   (b) a broom handle   (d) a handkerchief

11D Word Study

The prefix *com-* means "with." To *com*plain about something is to find fault with it. To make certain words easier to say, this prefix is sometimes written *con-*.

Complete the words below by providing the correct form of the prefix.

1. _____nect   to put together with

2. _____sume   to do away with or destroy

3. _____fident   pleased or satisfied with oneself

4. _____bine   to put one thing with another

5. _____patible   getting along with another

6. _____versation   a talk with someone

7. _____tent   satisfied with what one has

8. _____prehend   to understand or be familiar with

9. _____tact   get in touch with

10. _____panion   someone who travels with another

Read the passage below; then complete the exercise that follows.

Off You Go into the Wild Blue Yonder

After ten weeks of flying lessons, which is about the average instruction period, you are ready to take your first **solo** flight. Today, your instructor will be on the ground instead of sitting beside you. When you arrive at the airfield, you see her standing outside the **hangar**, and she greets you with a friendly wave. As the two of you chat, you try to sound as **nonchalant** as possible, even though your heart is pounding. She must see how nervous you are because she remarks that she has complete **confidence** in you. That makes you feel better, and you begin to relax a little as the two of you **saunter** over to the plane.

After climbing inside and taking a deep breath, you **methodically** complete the checklist of the plane's controls. Then, you wait for a signal from the control tower to **proceed**. As soon as it comes, your feelings of **anxiety** leave you. You start the engine and release the brake. You open the throttle a little, feeding more gasoline to the engine and causing the propeller to whirl faster. The plane starts to move forward. You taxi onto the runway, facing into the wind, and wait.

A voice from the control tower comes through your headphones, giving you permission to take off. You open the throttle wide, and the plane **accelerates** down the runway. Your right hand rests on the "stick," a control that lifts the plane's nose when pulled back and drops the nose when pushed forward. The plane is now traveling so fast that you can feel it trying to leave the ground. You pull back gently on the stick. The ground suddenly drops away beneath you. You are flying!

You have been told to go no faster than eighty-five miles an hour, although the plane has a **maximum** speed of twice that. You reach an **altitude** of five hundred feet and ease back on the throttle, watching your air speed carefully. If it drops below fifty-five miles an hour, the plane will **stall**. To increase speed, you push the stick forward, dropping the nose slightly. Already, it is time to make the first turn. You push the stick gently to the left, and the wing on that side drops, causing the plane to make a turn, or "bank" as you have learned to call it. There are so many things to think about that you hardly notice the view. After making three more left banks, you are on your final approach.

The control tower clears you for landing. You reduce the amount that the throttle is open and can feel the plane dropping. Not too fast. Not too steep an angle. Come in too high and you'll overshoot the runway; come in too low, and you'll fall short. You **brace** yourself as the runway comes rushing toward you.

When the plane is just inches off the ground, you close the throttle and pull back on the stick to raise the nose. Without power from the engine, the wings no longer support the plane, and it drops. You don't want to be too high when this happens or the plane will bounce as it makes **contact** with the ground. But you make a perfect landing. An **exultant** feeling sweeps over you as you roll down the runway and come to a stop. Flying is fun!

accelerate
altitude
anxious
brace
confident
contact
exult
hangar
maximum
methodical
nonchalant
proceed
saunter
solo
stall

Answer each of the following questions in the form of a sentence. If a question does not contain a vocabulary word from this lesson's word list, use one in your answer. Use each word only once. Questions and answers will then contain all fifteen words (or forms of the words).

1. What large airport building would be easily seen from the air?

2. What is the **maximum** speed allowed on the flight?

3. What is the meaning of **stall** as it is used in the passage?

4. What might happen if the check of the controls before a flight is less than **methodical**?

5. How does the pilot receive instructions when in the plane?

6. What is the meaning of **confidence** as it is used in the passage?

7. How does the pilot try to hide a feeling of nervousness before the flight?

8. How is it made clear that the pilot didn't hurry over to the plane?

9. What does the pilot need before **proceeding** to take off?

10. How much instruction is usually necessary before one is allowed to fly alone?

11. What happens to the plane's air speed when the nose drops slightly?

12. What happens to the plane when the pilot closes the throttle?

13. What is the meaning of **brace** as it is used in the passage?

14. How might the pilot **exult** after landing safely?

15. How might you feel if you were a pilot making your first flight alone?

FUN & FASCINATING FACTS

A plane's **altitude** is measured by an instrument called an *altimeter*, which shows the height above sea level, not the distance to the ground below. It does this by measuring the density of the air outside. It would show the same altitude, say 5,000 feet, over the ocean and over land that was 4,900 feet above sea level. In the second case, the plane actually would be barely skimming the ground.

Don't confuse **hangar**, a large building where aircraft are kept, with *hanger*, a metal, wood, or plastic frame on which clothes are hung. These two words are homophones.

The opposite of **maximum** is *minimum*. (For many years, most highways in the United States had a maximum speed of 55 m.p.h. and a *minimum* speed of 40 m.p.h.)

In Lesson 7, you learned several words formed from the Latin *solus*, which means "alone; without company." **Solo** is another of those words. A *solo* is an activity, musical or otherwise, performed by one person. A piece of music for two people is called a *duet*; for three people, a *trio*; and for four people, a *quartet*.

Lesson 12

Word List Study the definitions of the words below; then do the exercises for the lesson.

convalesce
kän və les´

v. To get back health and strength after an illness.
After the operation on my knee, I will **convalesce** at home.

dedicate
ded´ i kāt

v. 1. To set aside for a certain purpose.
My parents **dedicate** part of their income to saving for my college education.
2. To devote to a serious purpose.
Madame Curie **dedicated** her life to science.
3. To name, address, or set aside as an honor.
The authors **dedicated** the book to their two children.

dictate
dik´ tāt

v. 1. To give orders; to command.
The law **dictates** that children attend school until they are sixteen.
2. To say aloud while another writes down the words.
I **dictated** a letter to the manager of the company.
dictator *n.* A person who has complete control over a country; a person who is obeyed without question.
Hitler ruled Germany as a **dictator** from 1933 to 1945.

exasperate
eg zas´ pər āt

v. To make angry; to annoy.
My brother **exasperates** my parents because he uses the telephone so much.
exasperating *adj.* Very annoying.
Waiting in long lines to enter the stadium, before the game, can be quite **exasperating**.

notable
nōt´ ə bəl

adj. Deserving of attention; outstanding.
Eleanor Roosevelt was one of the most **notable** first ladies to occupy the White House.

overdue
ō vər dōō´

adj. 1. Coming later than expected or needed.
The bus from Boston is **overdue**.
2. Unpaid when owed.
My aunt never allows her bills to become **overdue**.

overthrow
ō vər thrō´

v. To end the rule of; to defeat, often by using force.
If we **overthrow** the king, who will take his place?
overthrew past tense.
The Polish people finally **overthrew** the Communist government that had been in power for more than forty years.
n. The action of overthrowing.
The **overthrow** of Anastasio Somoza, who ruled Nicaragua for many years, came in July 1979.

penetrate
pen´ ə trāt

v. 1. To pierce.
Luckily, the piece of glass Irma stepped on did not **penetrate** her foot.
2. To pass into or through.
Very little light **penetrated** the dense forest.

portrait
pôr´ trit

n. A drawing, painting, or photograph of a person, especially the face.
The famous **portrait** known as the Mona Lisa is in the Louvre, in Paris.

rebel
reb´ əl

v. To refuse to accept control by others.
The Philippine people **rebelled** against the government of Ferdinand Marcos.
n. A person who refuses to obey orders or the law.
If the **rebels** continue to gain popular support, they will be a serious threat to the government.
rebellious *adj.* (rē bel´ yəs) Fighting against another's control; disobedient.
Grounding is a punishment parents often use for **rebellious** teenagers.
rebellion *n.* (rē bel´ yən) Open opposition to another's control.
The Boxer **Rebellion** of 1900 was an attempt by the Chinese to throw foreigners out of the country.

restrict
rē strikt´

v. To keep within certain limits.
We **restrict** this pathway to people riding bicycles.
restriction *n.* A limit.
Our school has some **restrictions** about what students may wear.

seldom
sel´ dəm

adv. Not often; rarely.
Because the sun's rays are so strong, we **seldom** spend the whole day at the beach.

stimulate
stim´ yoo lāt

v. To make more active.
The aroma of black bean soup from the kitchen **stimulated** my appetite for lunch.

tempest
tem´ pəst

n. A violent windstorm usually with snow, rain, or hail.
A **tempest** at sea is a sailor's greatest fear.
tempestuous *adj.* Stormy, wild.
After a **tempestuous** exchange of views on global warming, the two scientists agreed to disagree and ended the discussion.

upbringing
up´ briŋ iŋ

n. The care and training a child gets while growing up.
In *Little Women*, Louisa May Alcott describes the **upbringing** of the four March sisters in nineteenth century New England.

convalesce
dedicate
dictate
exasperate
notable
overdue
overthrow
penetrate
portrait
rebel
restrict
seldom
stimulate
tempest
upbringing

12A Finding Meanings

Choose two phrases to form a sentence that correctly uses a word from Word List 12. Write each sentence in the space provided.

1. (a) end that person's rule by force.
   (b) To overthrow someone is to
   (c) To exasperate someone is to
   (d) serve under that person.

2. (a) is to put limits on it.
   (b) To restrict activity
   (c) To stimulate activity
   (d) is to prohibit it.

3. (a) If an event seldom happens,
   (b) it causes great excitement.
   (c) If an event is overdue,
   (d) it doesn't happen often.

4. (a) A notable scene   (c) is one that is delayed.
   (b) is one that is stormy.   (d) A tempestuous scene

5. (a) An upbringing is   (c) the time spent recovering.
   (b) A rebellion is   (d) a rising up against those in power.

6. (a) To stimulate someone is to   (c) annoy that person.
   (b) remove that person from power.   (d) To exasperate someone is to

7. (a) One's upbringing is   (c) the care one gets as a patient.
   (b) One's portrait is   (d) the care one gets as a child.

8. (a) is to name it in honor of someone.   (c) To dedicate a building
   (b) To penetrate a building   (d) is to tear it down.

9. (a) A dictator is   (c) a fight against control by others.
   (b) A portrait is   (d) a ruler with complete control.

10. (a) is made to oneself.   (c) An overdue pledge is one that
    (b) A notable pledge is one that   (d) should have been made earlier.

12B Just the Right Word

Improve each of the following sentences by crossing out the bold phrase and replacing it with a word (or a form of the word) from Word List 12.

1. You cannot use the movie pass on Sundays, but that is the only **limit placed upon its use**.

2. The arrow easily **passed through** the target.

3. This **painting which shows the face** of Queen Anne is three hundred years old.

4. While my arm was in a cast, I **had someone write down** what I wanted to say in my letters.

5. The **people who are fighting against their government** appear to be winning.

6. I recently discovered that one of my ancestors was quite **worthy of attention**.

7. After her hip operation, we brought my grandmother to our house to **get back her strength**.

8. Plenty of sunlight has **increased the activity of** my hibiscus plant to develop three new blossoms.

9. The Concord planetarium is **named after her as a way of showing respect** to Christa McAuliffe, who died aboard the *Challenger* space shuttle in January of 1986.

10. Trying to teach our dog to obey was an **unpleasant and very annoying** experience.

12C Applying Meanings

Circle the letter of each correct answer to the questions below. A question may have more than one correct answer.

1. Which of the following could be the subject of a **portrait**?
   (a) a hand
   (b) a child
   (c) the mayor of a city
   (d) a tree

2. Which of the following would help a person to **convalesce**?
   (a) quiet surroundings
   (b) fresh air
   (c) feelings of anxiety
   (d) a feeling of optimism

3. Which of the following could **penetrate** the skin?
   (a) a needle
   (b) a nail
   (c) a splinter of wood
   (d) a snowball

4. Which of the following are part of one's **upbringing**?
   (a) trees
   (b) parents
   (c) trips
   (d) cars

5. Which of the following might you do during a **tempest**?
   (a) stay home
   (b) seek shelter
   (c) go sailing
   (d) harvest crops

6. Which of the following can be **restricted**?
   (a) visits
   (b) dreams
   (c) parking
   (d) speech

convalesce
dedicate
dictate
exasperate
notable
overdue
overthrow
penetrate
portrait
rebel
restrict
seldom
stimulate
tempest
upbringing

7. Which of the following might cause people to **rebel**?

    (a) feelings of nostalgia   (c) feelings of desperation

    (b) harsh rule   (d) a harsh climate

8. Which of the following might be **exasperating**?

    (a) frivolous complaints   (c) airport delays

    (b) meddlesome cousins   (d) free gifts

12D Word Study

By adding, changing, or dropping a suffix, we alter the form of a word. The verb *act* becomes the adjective *active* when the suffix is added. The adjective *destructive* becomes the noun *destruction* when the suffix is changed. The noun *runner* becomes the verb *run* when the suffix is dropped. For each verb, noun, or adjective below, write in the two other forms of the word under the correct heading.

Verb	Noun	Adjective
1. _____	_____	navigational
2. rebel	_____	_____
3. _____	exasperation	_____
4. _____	_____	restrictive
5. _____	evasion	_____
6. _____	fascination	_____
7. _____	celebration	_____
8. _____	prosperity	_____
9. _____	_____	loathsome
10. obey	_____	_____

12E Passage

Read the passage below; then complete the exercise that follows.

A Child of the Revolution

When Frida Kahlo was born in Coyoacan, just outside Mexico City, in 1907, her parents probably thought her life would develop much as the lives of other girls of that time. The Mexican **dictator** Porfirio Diaz had been governing for almost thirty years, and under his rule women were **restricted** from taking any part in public life. Furthermore, Frida's parents gave her and her three sisters a strict Catholic **upbringing**. The girls were expected to be obedient daughters and to become good Catholic wives and mothers.

But in 1910, when Frida was three years old, everything changed in Mexico. The people **overthrew** Diaz and established a much more open government, which speedily set about making many changes that were long **overdue**. Education and health care became more widely available. More significantly for Frida Kahlo's future, the new government set out to **stimulate** interest in the arts by supporting the work of Mexican artists.

While her three sisters were largely unaffected by these changes, Frida, who was the **rebellious** one, took part in them. She seemed to enjoy shocking people. One of the ways she did this was to go about wearing men's clothes. Because she was a firm supporter of the 1910 revolution, as an adult she claimed to have been born that year so that she could call herself "a child of the revolution." Her Mexican mother and German father must have despaired of her at times, little knowing that their lively daughter would grow up to become one of Latin America's most **notable** painters.

Frida Kahlo had a difficult childhood. At the age of six she contracted polio, which left her with a weakened right leg. Then, in her late teens, she suffered terrible injuries when she was thrown from a bus onto a metal spike, which **penetrated** her side, almost killing her. While she **convalesced**, she began to paint. This was a way of taking her mind off the severe pain, from which she was **seldom** free for the rest of her life. Many of her paintings are self-**portraits**; in them she often included the parrots, monkeys, and other pets whose company gave her so much pleasure. Despite their bold, bright colors, however, the paintings clearly express the pain that lies behind them. Kahlo's art was her way of inviting the viewer to share her suffering.

She first met her future husband, the painter Diego Rivera, in 1922, when she was fifteen. They married seven years later. He was twice her age and already a world-famous artist. The marriage was a **tempestuous** one with many separations, a divorce, and later a remarriage. They both had strong personalities and each found the other **exasperating** to live with. Nevertheless, their love was strong and deep; Rivera appears frequently in her paintings.

Toward the end of her life, they lived together in the house where she was born, Casa Azul (the Blue House). After Kahlo's death in 1954, Rivera gave it to the people of Mexico. Now, known as the Frida Kahlo Museum, it is **dedicated** to her life and work.

convalesce

dedicate

dictate

exasperate

notable

overdue

overthrow

penetrate

portrait

rebel

restrict

seldom

stimulate

tempest

upbringing

Answer each of the following questions in the form of a sentence. If a question does not contain a vocabulary word from this lesson's word list, use one in your answer. Use each word only once. Questions and answers will then contain all fifteen words (or forms of the words).

1. What detail in the passage suggests that President Diaz was accustomed to being obeyed without question?

_____

2. How did the Mexican people show their dissatisfaction with President Diaz?

_____

3. How do you know that Kahlo's parents were not interested in experimenting with different ways of raising children?

_____

4. Why would Mexican artists have welcomed the 1910 revolution?

_____

5. Why do you think Kahlo's parents might sometimes have been **exasperated** with Frida?

_____

6. What is the meaning of **overdue** as it is used in the passage?

_____

7. In what way did Kahlo **rebel** against what was considered normal behavior?

_____

8. How do you think Kahlo's weakened right leg affected her life?

_____

9. Why did Kahlo probably lose a lot of blood in her accident?

_____

10. What helped Kahlo to **convalesce**?

_____

11. What is the meaning of **dedicated** as it is used in the passage?

12. How does the passage make clear that Kahlo never recovered completely from the accident?

13. Why would it be incorrect to describe Rivera and Kahlo as a compatible couple?

14. What did Frida Kahlo paint?

15. Why are both Diego Rivera and Frida Kahlo honored in the world of art?

FUN & FASCINATING FACTS

Dictate is formed from the Latin verb *dicere*, which means "to say" or "to speak." Other words formed from this root include *diction*, "a person's manner or way of speaking," and *contradict*, "to say the opposite of."

Three nouns are formed from the verb **stimulate**. *Stimulation* is the act of stimulating. (The aroma of freshly baked bread was the only *stimulation* we needed to enter the bakery.) A *stimulant* is a substance that increases bodily activity. (The caffeine in coffee and cola drinks is a *stimulant*.) A *stimulus* is anything that increases activity of any kind. (The reward of $50 was a *stimulus* to the children who were looking for the lost dog.)

Review for Lessons 9–12

Crossword Puzzle Solve the crossword puzzle below by studying the clues and filling in the answer boxes. Clues followed by a number are definitions of vocabulary words in Lessons 9 through 12. The number gives the lesson from which the answer to the clue is taken.

Clues Across

1. Not often (12)

4. A tied ball game goes into _____ innings

7. To chase after (10)

9. To walk in a relaxed, unhurried manner (11)

10. To copy closely (9)

11. To prepare; to make ready for a shock (11)

14. Opposite of "under"

15. To name or address as an honor (12)

17. To stop for a while before going on (9)

19. The state of being a slave (10)

21. To give to a fund or cause (10)

22. A building where aircraft are kept (11)

23. It covers the floor

24. One who watches an activity (9)

Clues Down

2. To keep away from (10)

3. Tightly packed; crowded close together (9)

5. A violent storm (12)

6. To go to a higher level (9)

7. To go on with after stopping for a while (11)

8. To fly high in the sky (9)

12. Opposite of "subtract"

13. To keep within certain limits (12)

14. Past the time set for arrival (12)

15. To give orders (12)

16. To get in touch with (11)

18. Planet known for its rings

20. Opposite of "sad"

Lesson 13

Word List Study the definitions of the words below; then do the exercises for the lesson.

accommodate
ə käm´ ə dat

v. 1. To have or to find room for.
This bus, which **accommodates** thirty adults, will drive to the historic buildings in the center of the city.
2. To do a favor for.
Tell me what you want, and I will try to **accommodate** you.

aggressive
ə gres´ iv

adj. 1. Ready to attack or start fights; acting in a hostile way.
Many animals become **aggressive** when their young are threatened.
2. Bold and active.
Rod Laver, the Australian tennis star, was an **aggressive** player at the net.

bask
bask

v. 1. To relax where it is pleasantly warm.
At lunch break, several students **basked** in the sunshine flooding the front steps.
2. To enjoy a warm or pleasant feeling.
The twins **basked** in the praise heaped on them by their parents.

carcass
kar´ kəs

n. The dead body of an animal.
New Zealand exports frozen lamb **carcasses** in refrigerator ships.

conceal
kən sēl´

v. To keep something or someone from being seen or known; to hide.
I **concealed** myself behind the curtain just as the thief entered the room.

flail
flāl

v. To strike out or swing wildly; to thrash about.
Matt's arms **flailed** desperately as he felt himself sinking into deep water.

gorge
gôrj

n. A narrow passage between steep cliffs.
We crossed the **gorge** on a swaying rope bridge.
v. To stuff with food; to eat greedily.
The children **gorged** themselves on watermelon at the family picnic.

morsel
môr´ səl

n. A small amount, especially of something good to eat; a tidbit.
For appetizers we served stuffed mushrooms and other tasty **morsels**.

protrude
prō trood´

v. To stick out; to project.
Watch out for the stone ledge that **protrudes** from the wall.

ripple
rip´ əl

v. To form small waves.
The breeze **rippled** the surface of the lake.
n. A movement like a small wave.
Raindrops made **ripples** in the pond.

slither slith´ ər	*v.* To move with a sliding, side-to-side motion of the body. A snake **slithered** through the grass.
sluggish slug´ ish	*adj.* 1. Lacking energy; not active. The heat made me **sluggish**. 2. Slow moving. In the dry season, the river becomes little more than a **sluggish** stream.
snout snout	*n.* The nose or jaws that stick out in front of certain animals' heads. The **snout** of a ferocious dog may need to be covered with a muzzle.
taper tā´ pər	*v.* 1. To make or become less wide or less thick at one end. A boning knife **tapers** to a very sharp point. 2. To lessen gradually. (Usually used with *off*.) As a loud knock was heard at the door, the speaker's voice **tapered** off, and she fell silent. *n.* A thin candle. The only light in the room came from a flickering **taper**.
visible viz´ ə bəl	*adj.* Able to be seen; exposed to view; not hidden. On a clear day Mount Shasta is **visible** from fifty miles away. **visibility** *n.* 1. The condition of being easily seen. An orange vest increases a cyclist's **visibility** on the road. 2. The distance within which things can be seen. **Visibility** is poor this morning because of the fog.

13A Finding Meanings

Choose two phrases to form a sentence that correctly uses a word from Word List 13. Write each sentence in the space provided.

1. (a) relax where it is pleasantly warm.   (c) To taper is to
   (b) move by sliding from side to side.   (d) To slither is to

2. (a) An aggressive animal is one   (c) that is a carnivore.
   (b) A sluggish animal is one   (d) that is ready to fight.

3. (a) stuff oneself with food.   (c) To gorge is to
   (b) strike out wildly.   (d) To taper is to

4. (a) a small wave.   (c) A carcass is
   (b) a tasty bit of food.   (d) A ripple is

5. (a) To flail is to
(b) To bask is to
(c) hold out one's arms.
(d) enjoy a pleasant feeling.

6. (a) within sight.
(b) To be visible is to be
(c) lacking energy.
(d) To be concealed is to be

7. (a) keep out of sight.
(b) To protrude is to
(c) strike out wildly.
(d) To flail is to

8. (a) an animal's slow movement.
(b) an animal's projecting nose.
(c) A morsel is
(d) A snout is

9. (a) speak favorably of that person.
(b) To conceal someone is to
(c) hide that person.
(d) To accommodate someone is to

10. (a) the body of a dead animal.
(b) a narrow passage.
(c) A carcass is
(d) A morsel is

accommodate

aggressive

bask

carcass

conceal

flail

gorge

morsel

protrude

ripple

slither

sluggish

snout

taper

visible

13B Just the Right Word

Improve each of the following sentences by crossing out the bold phrase and replacing it with a word (or a form of the word) from Word List 13.

1. The company received an avalanche of mail the first day, but the orders soon **began to arrive in smaller and smaller numbers**.

2. A leaf dropped onto the pond and **made small waves on** the surface.

3. The **narrow passage with cliffs on either side** is two hundred feet deep.

4. Will you be able to **find room for** all five of us in your car?

5. When a **small piece of something good to eat** fell to the floor, we let our dog eat it.

6. Customers who cannot pay their bills are pursued by the company in a very **active and forceful** manner.

7. The Inuit hunters cut up the **dead body of the animal** and shared it among themselves.

8. The twins **wildly swung** their arms and legs as their parents tried to dress them in snowsuits.

9. The tractor engine is **very slow to turn over** on these cold mornings.

10. Watch out! There are several rusty nails **sticking out** from that board lying on the ground in front of you.

13C Applying Meanings

Circle the letter of each correct answer to the questions below. A question may have more than one correct answer.

1. Which of the following would decrease **visibility**?
   - (a) fog
   - (b) a telescope
   - (c) a blizzard
   - (d) darkness

2. Which of the following is an **aggressive** remark?
   - (a) "Get out of my way!"
   - (b) "I'm sorry."
   - (c) "Forget it!"
   - (d) "Would you please repeat that?"

3. Which of the following might make a person **sluggish**?
   - (a) a heavy meal
   - (b) bracing air
   - (c) lying in the sun
   - (d) a stimulant

4. Which of the following animals **slither**?
   - (a) snakes
   - (b) lizards
   - (c) frogs
   - (d) kangaroos

5. Which of the following can **taper**?
   - (a) a twelve-inch ruler
   - (b) the blade of a dinner knife
   - (c) a candle
   - (d) the toe of a shoe

6. Which of the following **protrudes** from the head?
   - (a) the neck
   - (b) the nose
   - (c) the ears
   - (d) the brain

7. In which of the following places might one **bask**?

(a) on the beach   (c) near a campfire
(b) beside the pool   (d) on a tropical island

8. Which of the following might **accommodate** your neighbors?

(a) lending them your tools   (c) denouncing them to your friends
(b) inviting them to celebrate   (d) watching their house while they're away

13D Word Study

Look at each group of four words below containing two, three, or four synonyms. Underline any word that is *not* a synonym. To complete the exercise correctly, you may have to underline two, one, or no words.

1. aggressive   visible   hostile   friendly
2. taper   conceal   hide   obscure
3. exasperate   annoy   infuriate   protrude
4. anxious   worried   concerned   nervous
5. exultant   joyful   sluggish   methodical
6. absurd   nonchalant   silly   ridiculous
7. heroic   brave   fearless   bold
8. interest   fascinate   donate   attract
9. feeble   evasive   puny   burly
10. yearn   loathe   dislike   hate

accommodate
aggressive
bask
carcass
conceal
flail
gorge
morsel
protrude
ripple
slither
sluggish
snout
taper
visible

Read the passage below; then complete the exercise that follows.

Beware the Silent Crocodile

Crocodiles are the largest and most ferocious of all reptiles. They live in swampy areas, close to the banks of tropical rivers or lakes. They have been around since the age of the dinosaurs, when they reached lengths of thirty feet or more. The crocodile of today, however, is much smaller than its ancient ancestors, seldom growing longer than fifteen feet from its head to the tip of its long, **tapering** tail.

Crocodiles in the wild are almost unknown in North America. A few can be found in the remaining tidal marshes of the Everglades and the Florida Keys, where they might be mistaken for alligators, their close relatives. Although crocodiles and alligators resemble each other in many ways, there are clear differences between them. The crocodile is the more **aggressive** of the two. It also has a longer and narrower **snout**, and the fourth tooth on each side of its jaw **protrudes**, remaining in view even when its mouth is closed.

A crocodile in the water lies almost entirely **concealed** below the surface, with only its eyes and nostrils **visible**. It can stay like this for hours, its eyes fixed on the water's edge, waiting for a thirsty animal to come to drink. When this happens, the crocodile is careful not to scare away its prey. It disappears beneath the surface, swimming slowly toward the unsuspecting animal, without making the slightest **ripple**.

If the thirsty animal is lucky, it senses the danger in time and escapes. If the crocodile is lucky, it seizes the animal in its jaws, knocks it off balance by **flailing** its powerful tail, and drags it into the water, where the creature drowns. The crocodile then finds a place where it can **gorge** on the dead animal without being disturbed. When it has eaten its fill, it will hide the remains of the **carcass** and return to feed on it later.

When not hunting for food, the crocodile spends much of its time on land. Its belly almost touches the ground as it **slithers** from the water and finds a comfortable spot to **bask** in the sun. Like other reptiles, the crocodile is a cold-blooded animal; therefore, its temperature changes with its surroundings. To escape the extreme heat of midday, it burrows into the soft ground with its sharp claws until it has made a hole large enough to **accommodate** itself. In the cool of the evening, its temperature drops and its movements become **sluggish**.

There are several different kinds of crocodile. The best known is the Nile crocodile of Africa, which has an unusual companion called the crocodile bird. This daring little creature feeds by hopping inside the crocodile's mouth and picking **morsels** of meat from its teeth. The crocodile shows its gratitude for having its teeth cleaned in this way by not eating the bird.

Answer each of the following questions in the form of a sentence. If a question does not contain a vocabulary word from this lesson's word list, use one in your answer. Use each word only once. Questions and answers will then contain all fifteen words (or forms of the words).

1. Why is it unwise to get too close to a crocodile?

2. How does the shape of a crocodile's head differ from that of an alligator?

3. What do crocodiles and snakes have in common?

4. What is the shape of a crocodile's tail?

5. Why do crocodiles hide the **carcasses** of animals they have killed?

6. When are crocodiles likely to be slow in their movements?

7. What is the meaning of **bask** as it is used in the passage?

8. What parts of a swimming crocodile are **visible**?

9. How does a crocodile use its tail to overcome its prey?

10. What is the meaning of **accommodate** as it is used in the passage?

11. How does the passage suggest that a crocodile does not toy with its food?

12. Why is the prey of a crocodile unlikely to see it approaching in the water?

13. Why do you think the crocodile's eyes and nostrils **protrude** above the surface when it is in the water?

14. What do crocodile birds eat?

15. Why do crocodiles lie **concealed** in the water for long periods of time?

FUN & FASCINATING FACTS

A *slug* is like a snail but without the shell; it moves just about as fast as a snail, which is very slow indeed. *Slug* comes from an old Scandinavian word *slugje,* which means "a heavy, slow person." Both the noun *sluggard,* "a lazy, slow-moving person" and the adjective **sluggish** are formed from this word.

Don't confuse *tapir,* the name for a large piglike animal that lives in the forests of Central and South America, with **taper**. These two words sound the same but have different meanings and spellings. Can you remember what such pairs of words are called?

Lesson 14

> ## Word List
Study the definitions of the words below; then do the exercises for the lesson.

access
ak´ ses

n. 1. Freedom or permission to enter.
The students want **access** to the gym this summer.
2. A way of approach or entry.
The only **access** to the harbor is this channel.
accessible *adj.* Able to be used or entered.
Franklin's Restaurant is **accessible** to people in wheelchairs.

associate
ə sō´ shē āt

v. 1. To bring together in the mind.
Many people **associate** lobsters with Maine.
2. To come or be together as friends or companions.
Because of her love of racehorses, Anne often **associated** with others who shared that love—jockeys and trainers.
n. (ə sō´ shē ət) A person with whom one is connected in some way, as in business.
My father discussed the offer of a job in Chicago with his **associate** at work.

boisterous
bois´ tər əs

adj. Noisy and uncontrolled.
The Dixons' party became so **boisterous** that their neighbors complained.

brilliant
bril´ yənt

adj. 1. Very bright; sparkling.
My black patent-leather shoes had a **brilliant** shine.
2. Very clever or smart.
Einstein's **brilliant** mind was already evident in his youth.

decade
dek´ ād

n. A ten-year period.
Some people look back with nostalgia to the **decade** of the nineteen-sixties.

delicate
del´ i kət

adj. 1. Easily broken or damaged.
We always wash this **delicate** china by hand.
2. Needing care and skill.
Explaining someone's death to a small child is a **delicate** task.
3. In poor health; weak.
Although Isabella Bird Bishop was a **delicate** child, as an adult, she traveled through many different parts of the world, sometimes by canoe and other times on horseback.

employ
em ploi´

v. 1. To hire and put to work for pay.
Carmen's gift shop **employs** four people.
2. To use.
The clown **employed** every trick he knew to make the children laugh.

idle
ī´ dəl

adj. Doing nothing; not working.
The workers were **idle** while the power was shut off.
v. 1. To spend one's time doing nothing.
Last Sunday, while my brother **idled** for more than an hour in the house, I raked leaves in the yard.
2. To run (an engine) slowly.
Let the car **idle** for a few minutes so that the engine can warm up.

illuminate
il lōō´ mə nāt

v. 1. To light up; to supply with light.
The full moon **illuminated** the path through the woods to our cabin.
2. To make clear or understandable.
What you say about Goya's life **illuminates** this painting for me.

provide
prō vīd´

v. 1. To give what is needed; to supply.
Two local companies **provided** the money to buy our school band uniforms.
2. To set forth as a condition.
Our agreement with the company **provides** for three weeks of vacation time.

require
rē kwīr´

v. To need or demand.
Plants **require** light and water in order to grow.
requirement *n.* Something that is necessary.
A place to sleep and a simple meal were Johnny Appleseed's only **requirements**.

taunt
tônt

v. To make fun of in an insulting way; to jeer.
Don't **taunt** someone just because that person appears different.
n. An insulting remark.
An umpire learns to ignore the **taunts** of the crowd and just gets on with the job.

tolerant
tä́l´ ər ənt

adj. Willing to let others have their own beliefs and ways, even if different from one's own.
Traveling is both interesting and enjoyable if you are **tolerant** of customs that seem strange to you.
tolerate *v.* To accept willingly and without complaining.
You learn to **tolerate** a certain amount of noise when you live near an airport.

transform
trans fôrm´

v. To change the form, looks, or nature of.
A fresh coat of paint will **transform** this room.
transformation *n.* A complete change.
The **transformation** of the frog into a prince comes at the end of the story.

wilderness
wil´ dər nəs

n. An area where there are few people living; an area still in its natural state.
The Rocky Mountain states contain large areas of **wilderness**.

14A Finding Meanings

Choose two phrases to form a sentence that correctly uses a word from Word List 14. Write each sentence in the space provided.

1. (a) is unusually smart.
   (b) A delicate child is one who
   (c) A brilliant child is one who
   (d) is noisy and rough.

2. (a) give that person a job.
   (b) give that person a second chance.
   (c) To employ someone is to
   (d) To tolerate someone is to

3. (a) give it up.   (c) To require something is to
   (b) To provide something is to   (d) need it.

4. (a) Wilderness is   (c) a way of entering.
   (b) remoteness in space or time.   (d) Access is

5. (a) a business partner.   (c) A decade is
   (b) An associate is   (d) an insulting remark.

6. (a) to light it up.   (c) To transform a room is
   (b) To illuminate a room is   (d) to make it available.

7. (a) An idle person is one who is   (c) noisy and rough.
   (b) A boisterous person is one who is   (d) hard to talk to.

8. (a) a reassuring remark.   (c) A transformation is
   (b) A taunt is   (d) a complete change.

9. (a) one that runs sluggishly.   (c) one that is easy to get to.
   (b) An accessible machine is   (d) An idle machine is

access

associate

boisterous

brilliant

decade

delicate

employ

idle

illuminate

provide

require

taunt

tolerant

transform

wilderness

10. (a) is to put up with it.   (c) To tolerate something
    (b) To provide something   (d) is to do without it.

14B Just the Right Word

Improve each of the following sentences by crossing out the bold phrase and replacing it with a word (or a form of the word) from Word List 14.

1. Much of Alaska is **land that is still in its natural state** that needs to be protected.

2. In cold weather, let the engine **run slowly** for a few minutes before you drive anyplace.

3. Samantha hated school because some of her classmates **made fun of** her for the way she spoke.

4. The **ten-year period** that ended in 1929 was called "the Roaring Twenties."

5. These new curtains will **completely change the appearance of** this bedroom.

6. The matter is **one that needs careful handling**, but I am confident that you can take care of it.

7. This new health insurance will **make sure that you will be covered** for full payment of medical expenses.

8. This book **makes clear and understandable** how the two scientists figured out the structure of DNA.

9. I would be happier if my older sister were more **willing to overlook the faults of others** and less rigid.

10. One **thing that is necessary** to attend the new school is a uniform.

14C Applying Meanings

Circle the letter of each correct answer to the questions below. A question may have more than one correct answer.

1. Which of the following might an **idle** person do?
   (a) watch television
   (b) bask in the sun
   (c) win an Olympic medal
   (d) write a book

2. Which of the following could be a means of **access**?
   (a) a door
   (b) a wall
   (c) an opening
   (d) a window

3. Which of the following are closely **associated**?
   (a) baseball and summer
   (b) salt and pepper
   (c) Hansel and Gretel
   (d) snowflakes and cornflakes

4. Which of the following can be **brilliant**?
   (a) a diamond
   (b) an idea
   (c) moonlight
   (d) a student

5. Which of the following can be **delicate**?
   (a) a china plate
   (b) a problem
   (c) a rescue
   (d) a person's health

6. Which of the following is a **decade?**
   (a) the 1990s   (c) the 1700s
   (b) from 1901 to 1999   (d) 120 months

7. Which of the following might one find in a **wilderness?**
   (a) schools   (c) a herd of deer
   (b) trees   (d) a shopping mall

8. Which of the following would you not **tolerate?**
   (a) cheating   (c) crime
   (b) obedience   (d) prosperity

14D Word Study

The Greek word for "ten" is *deka*; it was borrowed by the Romans and became *deca*. Much later, the word was borrowed once again, this time by English-speaking people. It is found in several English words, among them *decade*, a period of ten years.

The names of several other Latin numbers have found their way into English words. Here are four of them:

mon or *mono* (one)   *bi* (two)   *tri* (three)   *quad* (four)

Use the Latin form of the numbers one, two, three, or four to complete each of the words below. If done correctly, each word will match the definition.

access
associate
boisterous
brilliant
decade
delicate
employ
idle
illuminate
provide
require
taunt
tolerant
transform
wilderness

1. _____angle   a figure with three straight sides

2. _____ruped   an animal with four legs

3. _____archy   rule by one person, a king or a queen

4. _____tonous   sounding just one note without varying

5. _____ped   a creature that walks upright on two legs

6. _____pod   a stand with three legs for supporting a camera

7. _____poly   control by one group over what is bought and sold

8. _____cycle   a vehicle with two wheels

9. _____ple   three times as many

10. _____ruple   four times as many

11. _____noculars   field glasses with two sets of lenses

12. _____rangle   an open space with four straight sides

14E Passage

Read the passage below; then complete the exercise that follows.

The Wizard of Menlo Park

Like other cities and towns in the late 1800s, New York City was a gloomy place at night. Streets were lit by flickering gas lights, if at all, and oil lamps or candles were all that people had to **illuminate** their homes. Thomas Edison had a better idea. In 1881, he built the world's first electric power station in Manhattan, helping to change New York into the **brilliantly** lit city we know today.

Edison was born in Ohio in 1847. When he was a small child, his family moved to Port Huron, Michigan. An attack of scarlet fever left him in **delicate** health. This worried his parents enough that they did not allow him to join in the **boisterous** games played at his school. The other children were not very **tolerant** of someone who stood apart from the rest, and young Edison had to suffer their **taunts**. His mother, who was a teacher, decided to take him out of school. She taught him at home, where he learned quickly. He asked many questions and liked to experiment on his own to find answers.

At that time, much of Michigan was **wilderness**, but the railroad was **transforming** America by making even the most remote places **accessible** to the rest of the country. When the railroad came to Port Huron, it **provided** Edison with his first job. At the age of twelve, he was given permission to sell newspapers and candy on the train that ran between his hometown and Detroit. He even printed his own newspaper, which he sold for three cents a copy.

At sixteen, he started working full-time on the railroad. For the next four years, he was **employed** as a telegraph operator in different towns. However, there were large portions of the day when he had nothing to do, and Thomas Edison hated to be **idle**. In addition, he **required** only five or six hours of sleep a night. So it was during this time that he began working on inventions along with his experiments.

At twenty-one, he invented an electrical vote counter, for which he was given a patent. This meant that the government identified him as the person who thought up the idea and protected it so that it could not be made or sold by others without his permission. When he was thirty, Edison established a research center at Menlo Park, New Jersey, where he and his **associates** ran what was really an inventions factory.

Over the next five **decades**, Edison was granted over a thousand patents by the United States government. Perhaps his most famous invention was the electric light bulb, but others included the record player (which he called a phonograph) and the movie camera. These things seemed like magic to people, so it isn't surprising that he became known as the "Wizard of Menlo Park." The once sickly child outlived most of his schoolmates—when he died in 1931, he was eighty-four years old.

Answer each of the following questions in the form of a sentence. If a question does not contain a vocabulary word from this lesson's word list, use one in your answer. Use each word only once. Questions and answers will then contain all fifteen words (or forms of the words).

1. How does the passage make clear that there were few towns in Michigan during Edison's youth?

2. In what way was the railroad important in Edison's early life?

3. With what invention do most people associate Edison?

4. What is the meaning of **illuminate** as it is used in the passage?

5. Why might Edison have been reluctant to go to school?

6. What **boisterous** activities might Edison's schoolmates have engaged in?

7. What details in the passage show that Edison's mother would not **tolerate** the behavior of Edison's classmates?

8. What is the meaning of **delicate** as it is used in the passage?

9. Why did Edison have **access** to the train from Port Huron to Detroit?

10. As a young man, how did Edison **employ** a lot of his free time?

11. What is the meaning of **idle** as it is used in the passage?

12. How did Edison change New York City?

13. How would you describe Edison's mind?

14. What must one do to protect a new invention from being copied by others?

15. How long did Edison live?

FUN & FASCINATING FACTS

Several nouns are formed from the verb **employ**. An *employee* is a person who works for someone else and is paid for this. An *employer* is a person who gives work to others and pays them. *Employment* is the state or condition of having work or the work itself.

Idle and *idol* are homophones. An *idol* is something, such as a carved figure, that is worshiped as a god. It can also be a person, such as a movie star or sports figure, who is greatly admired.

Illuminate comes from *lumen* the Latin word for "light." Other English words formed from this root include *luminous,* glowing with light, and *luminosity,* the amount of light given off, usually from within a thing itself, for example, a star. (The star with the greatest *luminosity,* apart from our own sun, is Sirius, also known as the Dog Star.)

Lesson 15

> **Word List** Study the definitions of the words below; then do the exercises for the lesson.

disaster
di zas´ tər

n. Something that causes great damage or harm.
Hurricane Katrina was the worst **disaster** to hit New Orleans in many years.
disastrous *adj.* Causing much damage or harm.
The **disastrous** floods in the Midwest left many people homeless.

flee
flē

v. To run away from danger or from something frightening.
I quickly decided to **flee** from the park when I heard a noise behind me.
fled past tense.
We **fled** from the house when we awoke and smelled gas.

fracture
frak´ chər

n. A crack or break, as in metal or bone.
The plane was grounded because of a small **fracture** in the metal tail unit.
v. To crack or break.
Ruth **fractured** her arm for the second time this summer when she fell from the swing.

immense
im mens´

adj. 1. Great in size or extent.
The Pacific Ocean is an **immense** body of water.
2. Great in degree.
To the **immense** relief of his parents, the lost child was soon found.

intense
in tens´

adj. 1. Very strong; very great.
The **intense** heat from the fire melted the plastic dishes.
2. Showing great depth of feeling.
The scene in the play where the slaves are liberated from bondage is so **intense** that the audience often weeps.
intensity *n.* Great strength or force.
The **intensity** of light from the sun is greatest at noon.

investigate
in ves´ tə gāt

v. To look into closely; to study in great detail.
The fire marshal will **investigate** the cause of the fire in the old mill.

lurch
lurch

v. To move forward or to one side suddenly and unexpectedly.
The car **lurched** to the left to avoid a pothole in the road.
n. A jerking or swaying movement.
The bus started with a **lurch**, throwing the standing passengers off balance.

major
mā´ jər

adj. Great in size, number, or importance.
Seas and oceans make up the **major** part of the earth's surface.
n. 1. A military officer just above a captain in rank.
A colonel is superior in rank to a **major**.
2. The main subject a student is studying.
My **major** in college will be Russian.
v. To study as one's most important subject.
My cousin Karen **majored** in chemistry and mathematics at Berea College.

minor
mī´ nər

adj. 1. Small; unimportant.
Steffi Graf's knee injury was **minor**, so she finished the match.
n. A person who is not yet an adult; a child.
Minors may attend this movie if an adult goes with them.

petrify
pe´ tri fī

v. 1. To make rigid with terror; to terrify.
The director said that he felt his horror movies had failed if they did not **petrify** audiences.
2. To change into a stonelike substance.
In Arizona's Painted Desert, we saw examples of wood that had **petrified** over millions of years.

predict
prē dikt´

v. To say what will happen before it takes place.
The state office on highway safety **predicts** heavy traffic on the roads this Labor Day weekend.
prediction *n.* Something that is predicted.
The **prediction** of a blizzard by the National Weather Service kept people from traveling last night.

prone
prōn

adj. 1. Likely to have or do.
All of us are more **prone** to colds in the winter than in the summer.
2. Lying face downward.
I had to lie in a **prone** position because my back was so sunburned.

sparse
spä´ rs

adj. 1. Thinly grown or spread.
The grass near the driveway was **sparse**, so we reseeded it.
2. Not crowded.
The town meeting had a **sparse** turnout this year.

topple
täp´ əl

v. 1. To fall or push over.
The cat **toppled** the pile of books.
2. To overthrow.
The student demonstrations helped to **topple** the government.

urban
ʉr´ bən

adj. Having to do with cities.
Traffic in **urban** areas is a serious problem during rush hour.

15A Finding Meanings

Choose two phrases to form a sentence that correctly uses a word from Word List 15. Write each sentence in the space provided.

1. (a) is one that is small and scattered.
   (b) A sparse crowd
   (c) is one that is very boisterous.
   (d) An immense crowd

2. (a) To investigate someone is to
   (b) terrify that person.
   (c) To petrify someone is to
   (d) come to that person's aid.

3. (a) An intense pain is one that   (c) A minor pain is one that
    (b) lasts for a long time.   (d) is very great.

4. (a) A prone figure is one   (c) that stands alone.
    (b) that is lying face down.   (d) A fleeing figure is one

5. (a) keep it from happening.   (c) look into it closely.
    (b) To predict an accident is to   (d) To investigate an accident is to

6. (a) a person who works in a mine.   (c) A minor is
    (b) a person who is not yet an adult.   (d) A major is

7. (a) To lurch is to   (c) lie in a facedown position.
    (b) To flee is to   (d) move forward suddenly.

8. (a) A prediction is   (c) a reminder of a past event.
    (b) A disaster is   (d) a forecast of what will happen.

9. (a) a student's main subject.   (c) A fracture is
    (b) a small wavelike movement.   (d) A major is

10. (a) An immense area is one   (c) that is very large.
     (b) An urban area is one   (d) that has few people.

disaster
flee
fracture
immense
intense
investigate
lurch
major
minor
petrify
predict
prone
sparse
topple
urban

15B Just the Right Word

Improve each of the following sentences by crossing out the bold phrase and replacing it with a word (or a form of the word) from Word List 15.

1. We **ran away** when the dog behind the flimsy gate started growling at us.

2. Much of the eastern United States that was wilderness in the 1700s is now **made up of cities and towns**.

3. The fire was a **terrible event that caused great damage**, but, fortunately, no lives were lost.

4. The car's **sudden movement** to the right told me we had a flat tire.

5. The **crack or break** in my arm took several weeks to heal.

6. The wood is millions of years old and has slowly **turned into a stonelike substance**.

7. The crossing guard's **first and most important** concern is the safety of the children as they are walking to school.

8. The **great force** of the speaker's words brought silence to the large crowd gathered for the memorial service.

9. Premature babies are **very likely** to suffer from lung problems.

10. The Mexican people **ended the rule of** President Diaz in 1910.

15C Applying Meanings

Circle the letter of each correct answer to the questions below. A question may have more than one correct answer.

1. Which of the following would you expect to see in an **urban** area?
   (a) farm animals
   (b) dirt roads
   (c) neon signs
   (d) skyscrapers

2. Which of the following could be **disastrous**?
   (a) an avalanche
   (b) a blizzard
   (c) an accomplishment
   (d) a voyage

3. Which of the following might one **predict**?
   (a) a person's age
   (b) a blizzard
   (c) the result of an election
   (d) the result of an experiment

4. Which of the following is a **minor** injury?
   (a) a scratched finger
   (b) a pulled muscle
   (c) a severed finger
   (d) a black eye

5. Which of the following is a **fracture**?
   (a) a broken leg
   (b) a broken promise
   (c) a broken heart
   (d) a broken arm

6. Which of the following would be visible on a **prone** person?
   (a) the stomach   (c) the back
   (b) the necktie   (d) the knees

7. Which of the following might one **investigate**?
   (a) a decade   (c) a crime
   (b) an explosion   (d) an accident

8. Which of the following can be **toppled**?
   (a) a tower   (c) a stack of books
   (b) a government   (d) a statue

15D Word Study

Write the antonym of each of the words on the left below in the space next to it. Choose from the words on the right, which are in a different order.

1. immense	_____	shy
2. major	_____	mild
3. brilliant	_____	obedient
4. delicate	_____	calm
5. idle	_____	tiny
6. conceal	_____	minor
7. seldom	_____	sturdy
8. confident	_____	dim
9. rebellious	_____	thick
10. tempestuous	_____	busy
11. intense	_____	reveal
12. sparse	_____	often

disaster

flee

fracture

immense

intense

investigate

lurch

major

minor

petrify

predict

prone

sparse

topple

urban

Read the passage below; then complete the exercise that follows.

When the Earth Quakes

Those who have lived through an earthquake describe it as one of the worst experiences of their lives. When one strikes, often without warning, people are usually too **petrified** to move. The ground, which a few moments before seemed so solid, suddenly **lurches** beneath their feet. Pictures are shaken from the walls, and if the earthquake is severe enough, the walls themselves may **topple.** Water and gas pipes burst, fires flare up, and lives may be lost.

The **intensity** of an earthquake is determined by a measure called the Richter scale. An earthquake measuring 4.0 is considered **minor**, causing little, if any, harm. One measuring 8.0 is more than one thousand times as powerful and can do **immense** damage. Another measure of the destructive power of an earthquake is the number of lives lost. One of the greatest natural **disasters** in history was the earthquake that struck China in 1556, killing almost a million people.

Earthquakes do the greatest damage in **urban** areas where people are concentrated. Most of the deaths and injuries occur when people are inside collapsing buildings. The San Francisco earthquake of 1906 measured 8.3 and killed 450 people; in 1964, Alaska, which is more **sparsely** settled, also experienced an earthquake measuring 8.3, but there were fewer than 200 deaths.

Scientists who **investigate** the causes of earthquakes are called seismologists. They have learned a great deal about these frightening occurrences. We know that the earth's crust or surface is made of rock five to twenty miles thick, which is **fractured** in many places. The separate pieces, or plates, fit more or less together along the break lines, which are known as "faults." Heat from the earth's interior puts pressure on these plates, causing them to move. Sometimes they rub against each other edge to edge; at other times one plate may ride up over another. These kinds of movements cause earthquakes.

Areas that lie along faults in the earth's crust are especially **prone** to earthquakes, but quakes can occur anywhere in the world. San Francisco lies on the San Andreas Fault, where the Pacific and North American plates meet. It has had two **major** earthquakes in the last century. The Pacific coast regions of Central and South America, where the Nazca and South American plates meet, have also suffered many earthquakes and will continue to do so.

Unfortunately, we still do not know enough about earthquakes to be able to **predict** accurately when one will occur. We do, however, make sure that today's buildings and bridges are strong enough to stand up to them. That is one reason why the 1989 San Francisco earthquake, which measured 6.9 on the Richter scale, took so few lives. But earthquakes are still to be feared. If you should have the misfortune to get caught in one, your first thought might be to **flee** to the nearest open space. Experts tell us, however, that if you are in a modern building, it is probably safer to stay inside. Look for shelter under a sturdy table or in a doorway.

Answer each of the following questions in the form of a sentence. If a question does not contain a vocabulary word from this lesson's word list, use one in your answer. Use each word only once. Questions and answers will then contain all fifteen words (or forms of the words).

1. What do seismologists do?

_____

2. What do the instruments used by seismologists measure?

_____

3. Why did scientists not know the 1989 San Francisco earthquake was coming?

_____

4. What urban area is on the San Andreas fault?

_____

5. What is the meaning of **topple** as it is used in the passage?

_____

6. What might cause people to fall during an earthquake?

_____

7. What is the meaning of **minor** as it is used in the passage?

_____

8. How might a person describe what it feels like to live through an earthquake?

_____

9. What would be the result of an earthquake in a city with many flimsy buildings?

_____

10. How serious would an earthquake measuring 7.8 on the Richter scale be?

_____

11. In what kind of area is an earthquake likely to do the least damage?

12. Why do you think streets are often flooded after an earthquake?

13. What is the meaning of **prone** as it is used in the passage?

14. How great was the loss of life in China's 1556 earthquake?

15. During an earthquake, when is it a good idea to **flee** to an open space?

FUN & FASCINATING FACTS

This is an *asterisk* (*). It looks like a star, and in fact the word comes from the Latin word for "star," which is *aster*. **Disaster** comes from the Latin prefix *dis-*, which means "against," and this Latin word for "star." But what does a disaster have to do with the stars? It was once believed (and still is, by some people) that the position of the stars had an effect on people's daily lives. If something bad (a *disaster*) happened to you, it was because the *stars* were *against* you.

Two other words formed from this same root are *astronomy*, the scientific study of planets and stars, and *astrology*, the belief that the stars have an effect on people's daily lives.

Flee and *flea* are homophones. A flea is a small jumping insect. **Minor** and *miner* are also homo-phones. A miner is a person who works in a mine, digging for coal, gold, or other minerals.

If you *break* a leg, you have a **fracture**. If you drop a cup it will *break* into *fragments*. If you *break* down the number 1 into smaller parts, such as halves or quarters, you get *fractions*. Something easily *broken* is *fragile*. All four of these words come from the Latin *frangere* or *fractus*, which means "to break."

The Latin prefix *pre-* means "before." A *premature* baby is one born *before* it is *mature* enough to leave the womb. Knowing this, and keeping in mind the explanation of *dictate* in Lesson 12 (page 98), you should be able to understand how **predict** is formed.

Lesson 16

Word List
Study the definitions of the words below; then do the exercises for the lesson.

abdicate
ab´ di kāt

v. To give up a high office.
When Edward VIII **abdicated** the throne in 1936, his younger brother became king of England.

assume
ə soom´

v. 1. To take for granted; to suppose.
We cannot **assume** that Mom and Dad will meet us at the station if the train is two hours late.
2. To take over; to occupy.
President Clinton **assumed** office on January 20, 1993.
3. To pretend to have.
Edin **assumed** a look of innocence when Vilma asked who had eaten the cookies.

bungle
buŋ´ gəl

v. To do something badly or without skill.
Because the shortstop **bungled** the double play, the runner made it safely to first base.

dominate
däm´ ə-nāt

v. 1. To rule or control; to have a very important place or position.
Rock **dominated** popular music in America for several decades.
2. To rise high above.
The Sears Tower **dominates** the Chicago skyline.

former
fôr´ mər

adj. Coming before in time; having been at an earlier time.
Three **former** mayors were invited to the dedication of our new city hall.
n. The first of two just mentioned.
Both the crocodile and the alligator are dangerous, but the **former** is more aggressive.

guardian
gär´ dē ən

n. 1. One who protects.
This ferocious dog acts as **guardian** of the property at night.
2. One who legally has the care of another person.
You need the permission of your parent or **guardian** to go on field trips.

hoist
hoist

v. To lift or raise, especially by using a rope.
The sailors **hoisted** the sails as we left the harbor.
n. Something used to lift, as a crane or pulley.
We cannot raise this unwieldy machine without a **hoist**.

intercept
in tər sept´

v. To stop or seize something while it is on its way somewhere.
The Coast Guard can **intercept** boats in United States waters to investigate their cargoes.

jubilee
joo´ bə lē

n. The celebration of an anniversary, especially a fiftieth anniversary or beyond.
The school marked its **jubilee** with a banquet for graduates from the past fifty years.

kin
kin

adj. Related by birth or marriage.
Are you **kin** to the Jordans or are you just a friend of theirs?
n. pl. (also **kinfolk**) Relatives; family.
She celebrated her ninetieth birthday with all her **kin** around her.
next of kin The person most closely related to someone.
The hospital requires the name of your **next of kin** when you are admitted.

pardon
pärd´ n

v. 1. To forgive.
Alice **pardoned** the Red Queen's rude remark.
2. To free from legal punishment.
The president of the United States has the power to **pardon** those convicted of crimes.
n. The act of forgiving or freeing from legal punishment.
A **pardon** can be controversial, as some people believe a convicted person should always serve out the full punishment.

proclaim
prō klām´

v. To make known publicly; to announce.
The mayor **proclaimed** May 18 a city holiday.

provoke
prō vōk´

v. 1. To annoy or make angry.
Josh said he took Katie's toys away because she **provoked** him with her constant talking.
2. To call forth; to rouse.
Senator Biden's comments **provoked** laughter in the audience.
provocative *adj.* (prō väk´ ə tiv) Calling forth anger, amusement, or thoughtfulness; trying to cause a response.
You were being **provocative** when you kept asking the same question over and over.

reign
rān

v. 1. To rule as a queen or king.
King Hussein of Jordan **reigned** for over forty years.
2. To be widespread.
Terror **reigned** in the streets of Paris during the French Revolution.
n. 1. The rule of a queen or king; the time during which a person rules.
The American Revolution occurred during the **reign** of George III.

riot
rī´ ət

n. 1. Public disorder or violence.
The 1992 **riots** in Los Angeles continued for several days.
2. A great and seemingly disordered quantity of something.
Catherine's rose garden is a **riot** of color in the summer.
v. To take part in a disorder.
As the crowd of townspeople **rioted**, the British soldiers opened fire.

16A Finding Meanings

Choose two phrases to form a sentence that correctly uses a word from Word List 16. Write each sentence in the space provided.

1. (a) To intercept something
   (b) To assume something
   (c) is to deliver it to its destination.
   (d) is to take it for granted.

2. (a) A pardon is
   (b) A jubilee is
   (c) a good deed that goes unrewarded.
   (d) a celebration to mark an anniversary.

3. (a) To riot is to
   (b) To reign is to
   (c) give up a position of responsibility.
   (d) take part in a public disorder.

4. (a) To hoist something is to
   (b) examine it closely.
   (c) seize it while it is on its way.
   (d) To intercept something is to

5. (a) control that person.
   (b) To pardon someone is to
   (c) forgive that person.
   (d) To provoke someone is to

6. (a) To be someone's guardian is to be
   (b) To be someone's kin is to be
   (c) friendly with that person.
   (d) related to that person.

7. (a) To reign is to
   (b) give up a high office.
   (c) rise to a higher level.
   (d) To abdicate is to

8. (a) whose work is in great demand.
   (b) A provocative speechwriter is one
   (c) who arouses interest or anger.
   (d) A former speechwriter is one

9. (a) lift it by using ropes.
   (b) make it widely known.
   (c) To bungle something is to
   (d) To hoist something is to

10. (a) To assume a position
    (b) To proclaim a position
    (c) is to take it over.
    (d) is to lie about it.

abdicate
assume
bungle
dominate
former
guardian
hoist
intercept
jubilee
kin
pardon
proclaim
provoke
reign
riot

16B Just the Right Word

Improve each of the following sentences by crossing out the bold phrase and replacing it with a word (or a form of the word) from Word List 16.

1. The hospital usually calls your **closest relative** if you are in an accident.

2. Are you trying to **stir things up and cause** a quarrel between your brothers?

3. Cleopatra **occupied the throne and ruled as queen** in Egypt from 51 B.C. to 30 B.C.

4. Singing this solo was my big chance to have a part in the musical, but I'm afraid I **didn't do a very good job of** it.

5. The painting's **seemingly disordered quantity** of color dazzles the eye.

6. Are you the **person legally named to act as parent** of this child?

7. September has been **publicly announced** "National Seafood Month."

8. After the fall of the Berlin Wall, many feared that Germany might **be much stronger than** the other countries of Europe.

9. Sometimes, Hope will **pretend to have** an Irish accent because she likes the way it sounds.

10. Labradors and collies are both good with children, but I prefer the **first of the two mentioned**.

16C Applying Meanings

Circle the letter of each correct answer to the questions below. A question may have more than one correct answer.

1. Which of the following could be **abdicated**?
   - (a) a high office
   - (b) an obstacle
   - (c) a school
   - (d) a throne

2. Which of the following would be your **kin**?
   - (a) your next-door neighbor
   - (b) your best friend
   - (c) your pet rabbit
   - (d) your uncle's wife

3. Which of the following might be **intercepted**?
   - (a) a message
   - (b) a tempest
   - (c) a ball
   - (d) a disaster

4. Which of the following might be **proclaimed**?
   - (a) a result
   - (b) a portrait
   - (c) a pardon
   - (d) a pledge

5. Which of the following might be **pardoned**?
   - (a) a mistake
   - (b) an insult
   - (c) a drought
   - (d) a rebel

6. Which of the following might **dominate** the skyline?

    (a) a tower   (c) a skyscraper

    (b) a lighthouse   (d) a stop sign

7. After what period of time might a **jubilee** be celebrated?

    (a) one year   (c) sixty years

    (b) fifty years   (d) one hundred days

8. Which of the following can one **assume**?

    (a) a leadership position   (c) a look of surprise

    (b) warm weather in the tropics   (d) the presidency

16D Word Study

The Latin prefix *pro-* is found at the beginning of a number of English words. It can mean "forward" or "onward" and sometimes "forth" or "in front."

Supply the missing word in each sentence below. All the words begin with the prefix *pro-*. Choose each word from the list given at the end of the exercise.

1. To _____ a boat is to make it go forward.

2. To _____ a rule is to set it forth hoping for its acceptance.

3. To _____ a rabbit out of a hat is to bring it forth in front of an audience.

4. To make _____ is to advance or go forward rather than backward.

5. To _____ a film is to throw the images forward onto a screen.

6. To _____ is to go forward, sometimes after stopping for a while.

7. To _____ the news is to say it out loud in front of a group.

8. To _____ one's tongue is to stick it out in front of one's face.

9. To _____ a response is to call it forth or bring it about.

10. To _____ for something is to set it forth as a condition.

abdicate

assume

bungle

dominate

former

guardian

hoist

intercept

jubilee

kin

pardon

proclaim

provoke

reign

riot

| protrude | proclaim | proceed | project | propel |
| produce | provide | provoke | propose | progress |

Read the passage below; then complete the exercise that follows.

The Last Queen of the Islands

Although she never dreamed it would happen, Liliuokalani grew up to become the queen of the Hawaiian Islands. Born on the island of Oahu in 1838, she was in her teens when her parents died. Her older brother Kalakaua became her **guardian**. They were **kin** to the Hawaiian royal family, but Kalakaua was not expected to succeed to the throne.

When King Lunalilo died in 1874, after ruling for barely one year, many believed that Queen Emma, widow of a **former** king, would be chosen to succeed him. It came as a surprise to Queen Emma's supporters that the elected members of Hawaii's governing body passed her by and **proclaimed** Kalakaua king instead.

King Kalakaua **reigned** for seventeen years. He had no children, so following the death of his younger brother in 1877, he chose Liliuokalani to succeed him to the throne. She ruled in her brother's place when he was absent from the kingdom and represented him at Queen Victoria's Golden **Jubilee** in London in 1887. The islands were **dominated** at that time by powerful planters and businessmen. Chief among them was Sanford Dole, a lawyer and a politician and the planters' natural leader. In 1887, this group forced Kalakaua to sign away almost all of his powers, making him Hawaii's ruler in name only.

Liliuokalani ascended the throne of Hawaii following her brother's death in 1891 and promptly set about regaining real power. The Hawaiian people resented the takeover of their government by the *haoles,* as the white-skinned Americans are called in Hawaiian. They supported their queen. When Liliuokalani declared a plan for government that gave more power to native Hawaiians, the *haoles* formed a committee to stop her. On January 16, 1893, the *haole* leaders brought in American sailors and marines, who were stationed on nearby ships, to prevent **riots** from breaking out in support of the queen.

The next day, the committee of *haoles* set up its own government with Sanford Dole as leader. Liliuokalani opposed this and asked the president of the United States for help. After an investigation, President Grover Cleveland ordered that Liliuokalani be returned to the throne. But Dole claimed that the U.S. government had no right to interfere in Hawaii's affairs, and on July 4, 1894, he **assumed** the presidency of the new Republic of Hawaii. Liliuokalani remained queen, but with no power to govern.

Early the next year, a group of Liliuokalani's supporters rebelled against the new government. The attempt was badly **bungled**, failing miserably. Dole accused Liliuokalani of **provoking** it and arrested her. Although she steadfastly denied being involved, messages between her and her followers had been **intercepted**, and weapons were found in her home. Liliuokalani was told that if she would **abdicate**, her supporters, who were then in jail, would not be put to death. To save their lives, she agreed to step down. She was sentenced to five years imprisonment for her role in the revolt. After eight months Dole **pardoned** her on the condition that she take no further part in politics, and she withdrew to her home, where she continued to fly the Hawaiian flag.

In 1898, Hawaii became part of the United States, with Sanford Dole serving as governor. During World War I, the first Hawaiians died fighting for the United States against Germany. The day she received the news, Liliuokalani lowered the Hawaiian flag and **hoisted** the Stars and Stripes.

Answer each of the following questions in the form of a sentence. If a question does not contain a vocabulary word from this lesson's word list, use one in your answer. Use each word only once. Questions and answers will then contain all fifteen words (or forms of the words).

1. What do you think was the significance of Liliuokalani's **hoisting** the Stars and Stripes?

2. What is the meaning of **guardian** as it is used in the passage?

3. What did Queen Emma expect to happen when Lunalilo died?

4. Why didn't Liliuokalani think about becoming queen of the Hawaiian Islands when she was a young girl?

5. Why was Queen Emma a very strong choice for ruler of Hawaii in 1874?

6. Why did Liliuokalani visit London in 1887?

7. Why couldn't President Cleveland **dominate** Sanford Dole?

8. Why were American sailors and marines brought to land in January 1893?

9. Why was Liliuokalani's situation so difficult when she was asked to **abdicate**?

10. What is the meaning of **assumed** as it is used in the passage?

11. Why did Dole's government continue to rule after the rebellion of 1895?

12. Why did the *haoles* claim that Liliuokalani took part in the 1895 uprising?

13. How did Liliuokalani respond when accused of being responsible for the 1895 rebellion?

14. What is the meaning of **pardoned** as it is used in the passage?

15. How many years was Liliuokalani queen before Hawaii became a republic?

FUN & FASCINATING FACTS

The antonym of **former** is *latter*. If given a choice between silk and cotton, and you choose the *latter*, you will get cotton. If you choose the *former*, you will get silk.

The Latin prefix *inter-* means "between." International affairs are those conducted *between* nations; *interstate* commerce is business conducted *between* states. This prefix is combined with the root from the Latin verb *capere*, "to take," to form the word **intercept**. Something that is *intercepted* is *taken* as it passes *between* the sender and the receiver.

Jubilee has an interesting story behind it. It comes from the Hebrew *yobhel*, which was a ram's horn used as a trumpet. It was blown every fifty years to celebrate the release of the Jews from bondage.

The word applies especially to a fiftieth anniversary but is used to mark other anniversaries as well. In 1897, Queen Victoria celebrated her Diamond Jubilee, by which time she had occupied the British throne for sixty years.

Homophones usually come in pairs but sometimes come in threes. *Reign, rain,* and *rein* are homophones. To rein in a horse is to control its speed by pulling on the reins.

Review for Lessons 13–16

Crossword Puzzle Solve the crossword puzzle below by study-ing the clues and filling in the answer boxes. Clues followed by a number are definitions of vocabulary words in Lessons 13 through 16. The number gives the lesson from which the answer to the clue is taken.

Clues Across

1. To fall over (15)

5. Able to be seen; within view (13)

9. Upset or angry

10. A violent public disorder (16)

11. Something that causes great damage (15)

13. To run from danger (15)

14. To make known publicly (16)

17. To say what will happen before it takes place (15)

23. To seize something while it is on its way (16)

25. One who protects (16)

26. To have

27. Opposite of "in front of"

28. Worn to protect the head

29. Adam and _____

Clues Down

2. To make angry (16)

3. Opposite of "begin"

4. To take for granted (16)

6. Showing great depth of feeling (15)

7. To hire and put to work for pay (14)

8. To do nothing (14)

10. A small wave (13)

12. To need (14)

15. A partner in business (14)

16. To stick out (13)

18. The rule of a queen or king (16)

19. A tasty tidbit (13)

20. A person who is not yet an adult (15)

21. A ten-year period (14)

22. To move suddenly and unexpectedly (15)

24. To become less wide at one end (13)

Lesson 17

Word List

Study the definitions of the words below; then do the exercises for the lesson.

afflict
ə flikt´

v. To bring or cause pain and suffering.
The patient has been **afflicted** with swollen feet for several months.
affliction *n.* A condition of pain, suffering, or trouble.
Frida Kahlo's **affliction** was the result of a serious accident.

barren
bar´ ən

adj. Not fruitful; not reproducing.
When the topsoil is washed away, the land is **barren**.

consist
kən sist´

v. To be made up; to contain.
The wedding banquet will **consist** of six courses.

drought
drout

n. A long period without rain.
The poor harvest was due to the **drought**.

erode
ē rōd´

v. To wear away bit by bit; to wear away by action of wind, water, or ice.
Heavy seas from yesterday's storm have **eroded** parts of the cliff.
erosion *n.* The process or state of eroding.
Cutting down many trees in one area leads to soil **erosion**.

expand
ek spand´

v. 1. To make or become larger.
You can **expand** your chest by taking a very deep breath.
2. To give further details of.
Mr. da Silva asked me to **expand** on some of the information in my report.
expansion *n.* The act, process, or result of enlarging.
Ten new employees were hired as a result of the company's **expansion**.

famine
fam´ in

n. A widespread and long-lasting shortage of food that may cause starvation.
The **famine** in Somalia was the result of several poor harvests in a row.

fertile
furt´ l

adj. 1. Able to produce good crops.
The major reason we grow such large tomatoes is the **fertile** soil.
2. Able to produce offspring.
A female cat is **fertile** at six months.
3. Able to produce ideas; inventive.
Many ideas sprang from Edison's **fertile** brain.

oasis
ō ā´ sis

n. **oases** *n. pl.* (ō ā´ sēz) A place where there is water in an otherwise dry area.
Travelers across the Sahara try to reach the next **oasis** before nightfall.

pasture
pas´ chər

n. A field of growing grass where animals can eat; a meadow.
We put the sheep in a different **pasture** to give the grass in this one a chance to grow back.
v. To put animals out in a field to eat grass.
We **pasture** our horses on a neighbor's land.

133

primitive prim´ i tiv	*adj.* 1. From earliest times; ancient. The **primitive** cave drawings at Lascaux, France, are over fifteen thousand years old. 2. Simple or crude. The Weinsteins replaced the **primitive** shed behind the house with a modern garage.
refuge ref´ yōoj	*n.* 1. Shelter or protection from harm. The hikers found **refuge** from the blizzard in a nearby cave. 2. A place of safety. During the hurricane, families living in beach houses found **refuge** in the high school gym. **refugee** *n.* A person forced to leave her or his home or country seeking protection from danger. A camp for Kurdish **refugees** was set up between Turkey and Iraq.
revert rē vurt´	*v.* To go back to an earlier condition, often one that is not as satisfactory. During the week that the electric power lines were being repaired, we **reverted** to eating our meals by candlelight and lantern.
teem tēm	*v.* To be filled; to occur in large numbers. The Columbia River once **teemed** with salmon.
wither with´ ər	*v.* To become dried out; to lose freshness. The crops will **wither** unless we have rain soon.

17A Finding Meanings

Choose two phrases to form a sentence that correctly uses a word from Word List 17. Write each sentence in the space provided.

afflict
barren
consist
drought
erode
expand
famine
fertile
oasis
pasture
primitive
refuge
revert
teem
wither

1. (a) go beyond what is permitted.
   (b) To expand is to
   (c) To erode is to
   (d) gradually wear away.

2. (a) a place with water in an otherwise dry area.
   (b) a condition from which one suffers.
   (c) An oasis is
   (d) A pasture is

3. (a) give more details about it.
   (b) To expand on something is to
   (c) To revert to something is to
   (d) mention it for the first time.

4. (a) To consist of something is to
   (b) To teem with something is to
   (c) be made up of it.
   (d) be associated with it.

5. (a) To wither is to
   (b) continue to improve.
   (c) go back to an earlier condition.
   (d) To revert is to

6. (a) a place of safety in time of danger.   (c) A drought is
   (b) a grassy area where animals feed.   (d) A pasture is

7. (a) To wither is to   (c) dry out from lack of water.
   (b) To teem is to   (d) sink to a lower level.

8. (a) A famine is   (c) a long period without rain.
   (b) A drought is   (d) an area where little can grow.

9. (a) An expansion is   (c) An affliction is
   (b) a place of great danger.   (d) a condition causing suffering.

10. (a) A refuge is   (c) a person in poor health.
    (b) a place of safety.   (d) A famine is

17B Just the Right Word

Improve each of the following sentences by crossing out the bold phrase and replacing it with a word (or a form of the word) from Word List 17.

1. Al Kufrah is a well-known **place where water is found in an otherwise dry area** in Libya.

2. When children taunted her, it led to the **gradual wearing away** of her confidence.

3. The way the villagers draw water from the river may be **the same as that used in very early times**, but it is quite effective.

4. If the cow you bought is not **capable of producing calves**, the dealer will return the money you paid for it.

5. Our breakfast usually **is made up** of cereal, milk, fruit, and coffee.

6. Because the number of children taking tennis lessons is **growing larger** every year, we now offer three sessions during the summer.

7. Acid rain destroys lakes that once **were filled** with fish.

8. President Roosevelt was **made to suffer when he came down** with polio at the age of thirty-nine.

9. We **provide grass for** our goats in a neighbor's field.

10. Many **persons fleeing for their safety** from Nazi Germany came to the United States in the 1930s.

17C Applying Meanings

Circle the letter of each correct answer to the questions below. A question may have more than one correct answer.

1. Which of the following might **wither**?
   - (a) crops
   - (b) trees
   - (c) leaves
   - (d) beaches

2. Which of the following could one **expand**?
   - (a) one's knowledge
   - (b) one's age
   - (c) one's home
   - (d) one's chest

3. Which of the following can result from **famine**?
   - (a) despair
   - (b) sickness
   - (c) death
   - (d) hunger

4. Which of the following can be **barren**?
   - (a) a goat
   - (b) a valley
   - (c) a pear tree
   - (d) a pasture

5. Which of the following might occur during a **drought**?
   - (a) restrictions on water use
   - (b) forest fires
   - (c) a yearning for rain
   - (d) flooding

6. Which of the following can be **fertile**?
   - (a) a kitten
   - (b) soil
   - (c) a mind
   - (d) a morsel

7. Which of the following might one find in a **pasture**?
   - (a) cargo
   - (b) cows
   - (c) sheep
   - (d) grass

8. Which of the following can be **eroded**?
   - (a) soil
   - (b) confidence
   - (c) cliffs
   - (d) savings

afflict
barren
consist
drought
erode
expand
famine
fertile
oasis
pasture
primitive
refuge
revert
teem
wither

17D Word Study

Words that have different meanings and different spellings but sound the same are called homophones. *Sore* and *soar* are homophones.

Read the pairs of sentences below. Then choose the homophone that best fits each sentence.

idol/idle

1. We didn't _____, as we wanted to finish our chores quickly.

2. The _____ was made of gold with rubies for its eyes.

taper/tapir

3. The _____ was dripping wax onto the table.

4. The _____ is an animal with a long, flexible snout.

teem/team

5. The streets _____ with tourists during the summer months.

6. May the best _____ win.

reigns/reins

7. The chart lists the _____ of all the English kings and queens.

8. The _____ are used to control the horse.

barren/baron

9. The Sahara is _____ except for the occasional oasis.

10. A _____ can sit in the British House of Lords.

minor/miner

11. In the U.S., anyone under eighteen is considered a _____.

12. Every gold _____ in California hoped to strike it rich.

flee/flea

13. A _____ can jump many times its height.

14. Most people were able to _____ inland before the hurricane struck.

hanger/hangar

15. The aircraft was wheeled out of the _____.

16. I put the coat on a _____ and hung it in the closet.

17E Passage

Read the passage below; then complete the exercise that follows.

A Harvest of Sand

The ability of the earth to support life depends on the amount of rainfall it receives. The tropical rain forests of Africa, Asia, and Central and South America, which are **teeming** with life, get up to four hundred inches a year. Yet in other parts of the world, little or no rain falls, making the land **barren**. Areas where the annual rainfall is less than ten inches a year are called deserts.

The largest of the earth's deserts is the Sahara, in northern Africa, which covers an area almost as big as the United States. Apart from the central portion, which is mountainous, the Sahara **consists** mostly of sand. There is water, but it lies far below the surface in ancient underground lakes. In some places it bubbles to the surface in the form of springs. More often, though, wells have to be dug to get to it. In these places the soil is **fertile**, and people can grow crops and raise animals. **Oases** spring up around these places, often becoming the size of small towns. They are a welcome sight to the travelers who cross this harsh land on the backs of camels, or more commonly today, in four-wheel-drive vehicles.

South of the Sahara are the countries that make up the Sahel, an area that stretches four thousand miles from Senegal in the west to Ethiopia in the east. This part of Africa was once mostly grassland that provided good pasture for cattle and made it possible for the people of these countries to be reasonably well fed. In recent years, however, it has been afflicted with long dry spells, the worst in nearly two centuries. As the droughts continue, rivers and lakes dry up; without water, the grass withers and the cattle are left with nothing to feed on. To make matters worse, too many trees that held the soil in place have been cut down for firewood, resulting in widespread soil **erosion**.

Because of changing weather patterns, the Sahara is spreading into the Sahel. As it continues to **expand** southward, the Sahara has taken over more than a quarter of a million square miles since the 1950s. This is equivalent to an area roughly the size of France and Austria combined. Although nothing can be done to change weather patterns, scientists believe that in time conditions will change, and the land that is now desert may **revert** to grassland.

The people of the Sahel have suffered greatly, however. Hundreds of thousands have already died as a result of **famine**, and one third of all the children born in the Sahel still die before their fifth birthdays. Millions have left their once prosperous villages and have poured into the overcrowded cities to the south, where they live in **primitive** shelters. Nouakchott, on Africa's west coast, was home to fifteen thousand people in the 1950s. By 2004, the town's population had exploded to six hundred thousand people, most of them **refugees** from the slowly spreading desert to the north.

afflict

barren

consist

drought

erode

expand

famine

fertile

oasis

pasture

primitive

refuge

revert

teem

wither

Answer each of the following questions in the form of a sentence. If a question does not contain a vocabulary word from this lesson's word list, use one in your answer. Use each word only once. Questions and answers will then contain all fifteen words (or forms of the words).

1. Why are deserts **barren** places?

2. What happens to the people of the Sahel who are driven from their land?

3. Where is it possible to grow crops in the Sahara?

4. How has the Sahara changed in recent years?

5. What is the meaning of **fertile** as it is used in the passage?

6. In what way do tropical rain forests differ from deserts?

7. What is the main cause of **drought** in the Sahel?

8. What is the meaning of **primitive** as it is used in the passage?

9. How are cattle affected by the worsening conditions in the Sahel?

10. What happens to plants that don't get enough water?

11. Why does the cutting down of trees lead to soil **erosion**?

12. Why do scientists think that the Sahel may not remain a desert?

13. How does the present dry spell in the Sahel compare with those in the past?

14. Why would the Sahara have a brownish color when seen from space?

15. How can food shipments from outside help the people of the Sahel?

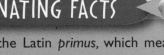

FUN & FASCINATING FACTS

To **afflict** is to cause pain and suffering. To *inflict* (Word List 6) is to cause something damaging or painful to be felt. If you are confused by the similarity in meaning of these two words, you are not alone. The difference between them is that *afflict* deals with what is *felt*, whereas *inflict* with what is *done*. In the sentence "The judge *inflicted* a severe sentence," the judge *did* something. In the sentence "The prisoner was *afflicted* with guilt," the prisoner *felt* something.

Barren and *baron* are homophones. A *baron* is a nobleman. It was the English barons who, in 1215, forced King John to sign the Magna Carta, granting civil rights to English citizens.

Primitive tools, which may be tens of thousand of years old, are found buried in many parts of the world. They are among the first tools made by humans, as the word *primitive* suggests. It comes from the Latin *primus,* which means "first." A number of other English words share this root. A *primary* reason is one that comes *first* in importance; a *primer* is a book of *first* instruction in a subject; and a *prime* minister in many countries is the leader who is *first* in importance.

Teem and *team* form another pair of homophones. A team is a group of people who play or work together.

Wither, a verb, should not be confused with the adverb *whither*, meaning "to what place; where." These two words are not homophones because the "h" in *whither* is sounded. *Whither* is a poetic word that is falling out of use. Once when people wished to know where someone was going, they would ask, "Whither are you going?" or "Whither goest thou?"

Lesson 18

Word List
Study the definitions of the words below; then do the exercises for the lesson.

animated
an´ ə māt əd

adj. 1. Alive or seeming to be alive.
The movie combines **animated** cartoon figures with live actors.
2. Full of energy; lively.
The class discussion became quite **animated** when we talked about raising the driving age.

betray
bē trā´

v. 1. To be disloyal to.
Members of the Underground Railroad could be counted on not to **betray** escaping slaves to their owners.
2. To show; to reveal.
Jonas insisted that he wasn't upset, but his tears **betrayed** his true feelings.

convince
kən vins´

v. To make someone feel sure or certain; to persuade.
I tried to **convince** my parents that I was old enough to be left alone in the house.

decline
dē klīn´

v. 1. To slope or pass to a lower level.
The path **declines** sharply here, then rises.
2. To refuse to accept.
Olga **declined** my offer of a ride to school because she wanted to walk.
3. To become less or weaker.
Tiny Tim's health could **decline**, the ghost told Scrooge, if no one did anything to help.
n. 1. A change to a smaller amount or lower level.
The **decline** in attendance at the ballpark worries the team's owners.
2. A loss of strength or power.
The **decline** of the Roman Empire is the subject of a famous book by Edward Gibbon.

hilarious
hi lar´ ē əs

adj. Very funny.
The comedian's **hilarious** jokes had us all in stitches.

likeness
līk´ nəs

n. The state of being similar; something that is similar.
Your **likeness** to your sister is remarkable.

meager
mē´ gər

adj. Poor in quality or insufficient in amount.
A stale crust of bread makes a **meager** meal.

mischief
mis´ chif

n. 1. Harm or damage.
Our neighbor's meddling in other people's affairs caused a lot of **mischief**.
2. Behavior that causes harm or trouble.
Their **mischief** during class will get them in trouble.
3. Playfulness; harmless amusement.
Hiding her mother's hat was just the child's **mischief**.
mischievous *adj.* (mis´ chə vəs) Playful in a naughty way.
The **mischievous** cat pawed at the dog's tail.

negotiate
ni gō´ shē āt

v. 1. To arrange by talking over.
The teachers are meeting with the school board to **negotiate** a new contract.
2. To travel successfully along or over.
This slope has some difficult sections that only accomplished skiers can **negotiate**.

obsolete
äb sə lēt´

adj. No longer sold or in wide use because it is out-of-date.
Compact discs made records nearly **obsolete**.

retain
rē tān´

v. 1. To hold onto; to keep possession of.
Because of today's victory, we **retained** our position at the top of the girls' hockey league.
2. To hire the services of.
The airline **retained** its own safety experts to investigate the wing fractures.

sensation
sen sā´ shən

n. 1. A feeling that comes from stimulation of the senses.
Drinking hot cocoa after two hours of sledding gave us a warm **sensation**.
2. A feeling of great interest or excitement or the cause of such a feeling.
The appearance at our school of the basketball star caused a **sensation**.
sensational *adj.* 1. Causing great curiosity and interest.
The **sensational** headline led me to buy the newspaper.
2. Very great or excellent.
With your quick mind, you'll make a **sensational** addition to the debating team.

somber
säm´ bər

adj. 1. Dark; gloomy.
We began our hike under a **somber** sky; fortunately, the sun came out in the afternoon.
2. Sad; serious.
Grandfather's death put us in a **somber** mood.

subsequent
sub´ sə kwənt

adj. Coming later; following.
The first book in the series was a disappointment, but **subsequent** ones have been very enjoyable.

vow
vou

v. To promise seriously.
The rescue workers **vowed** to continue working until all those trapped in the building were freed.
n. A pledge; a promise.
When my parents became citizens of the United States, they made a **vow** to support this country.

animated
betray
convince
decline
hilarious
likeness
meager
mischief
negotiate
obsolete
retain
sensation
somber
subsequent
vow

18A Finding Meanings

Choose two phrases to form a sentence that correctly uses a word from Word List 18. Write each sentence in the space provided.

1. (a) A hilarious story is
   (b) A mischievous story is
   (c) one that could cause trouble.
   (d) one that expresses optimism.

2. (a) An animated speech is
   (b) one that is very lively.
   (c) A somber speech is
   (d) one that is reassuring.

3. (a) To convince someone is to
   (b) make a promise to that person.
   (c) persuade that person.
   (d) To betray someone is to

4. (a) A sensation is   (c) a serious promise.
   (b) A vow is   (d) a serious weakness.

5. (a) To betray someone   (c) is to avoid that person.
   (b) To negotiate with someone   (d) is to be disloyal to that person.

6. (a) To retain a lawyer's services   (c) To decline a lawyer's services
   (b) is to decide not to use them.   (d) is to terminate them.

7. (a) one that is very funny.   (c) An obsolete form of entertainment is
   (b) one that costs a lot of money.   (d) A hilarious form of entertainment is

8. (a) To retain a contract is to   (c) arrange it by talking it over.
   (b) To negotiate a contract is to   (d) sign it.

9. (a) that causes great excitement.   (c) A meager costume is one
   (b) A sensational costume is one   (d) that is no longer in use.

10. (a) A subsequent meeting   (c) A somber meeting
    (b) is one that provokes laughter.   (d) is one that is very serious.

18B Just the Right Word

Improve each of the following sentences by crossing out the bold phrase and replacing it with a word (or a form of the word) from Word List 18.

1. My parents **hired the services of** a tutor to help me with my math.

2. Ten dollars seems a **very small** amount for doing such a lot of work.

3. Dial telephones are now **no longer used very much**.

4. When I met Sara's brother, I immediately noticed his **similarity in appearance** to her.

5. His nervous glances at the clock **gave away** his attempt to hide his anxiety.

6. The Cuddlibear was a **cause of great excitement** at the toy fair.

7. **Traveling successfully over** the icy road during the snowstorm was a challenge for me.

8. Reporting false emergencies to the police and similar **behavior that causes trouble** will result in severe punishment.

9. We discussed the matter at a **meeting that took place after the first** meeting.

10. Angela **made a serious promise** to be more patient with her younger brother.

18C Applying Meanings

Circle the letter of each correct answer to the questions below. A question may have more than one correct answer.

1. Which of the following can one **retain**?
   (a) a lawyer
   (b) one's pride
   (c) one's youth
   (d) one's memories

2. Which of the following can be a **sensation**?
   (a) warmth
   (b) cold
   (c) ice
   (d) fire

3. Which of the following is a **somber** color?
   (a) bright red
   (b) dark green
   (c) pale pink
   (d) deep brown

4. Which of the following might **decline**?
   (a) a pathway
   (b) one's health
   (c) prices
   (d) winter

5. Which of the following could one **betray**?
   (a) one's true feelings
   (b) a trust
   (c) one's country
   (d) one's friends

6. Which of the following might one **vow** to do?
   (a) sneeze
   (b) love someone
   (c) protect someone
   (d) go shopping with someone

animated
betray
convince
decline
hilarious
likeness
meager
mischief
negotiate
obsolete
retain
sensation
somber
subsequent
vow

7. Which of the following is **animated**?

    (a) a carcass   (c) a cartoon film

    (b) a sleeping child   (d) a comic book

8. Which of the following is likely to cause **mischief**?

    (a) reassuring a classmate   (c) helping a friend

    (b) provoking a quarrel   (d) taunting a companion

18D Word Study

Synonyms are words that have the same or similar meaning. This means that writers are always having to make choices. Which of several words with similar meaning is the right one? The good writer chooses the one that belongs in the sentence better than any of its synonyms.

Here are five words that have the same or similar meaning:

    disturbance   **rebellion**   **riot**   **uprising**   **uproar**

Complete the following sentences by writing each of these words in the space where you think it fits best.

1. The prison _____ ended peacefully after the governor met with the inmates.

2. The _____ began with an attack on the presidential residence.

3. The person who caused the _____ was asked to leave the lecture hall.

4. President Washington sent troops to put down the 1794 _____.

5. When the mouse escaped, it caused a(n) _____ in the classroom.

Here are five more words that have the same or similar meaning:

    sore   **tender**   **aching**   **painful**   **agonizing**

Complete the following sentences by writing each of these words in the space where you think it fits best.

6. The doctor pressed the patient's abdomen to see if it felt _____.

7. A(n) _____ tooth may be the first sign of a cavity.

8. Soaking in a hot tub helps to ease _____ muscles.

9. It is very _____ when I try to walk on my injured ankle.

10. A severe burn can be _____ for the victim.

Read the passage below; then complete the exercise that follows.

A Mouse Is Born

In 1927, Walt Disney worked in the movie business, producing short **animated** cartoons. He had started his own film company in Los Angeles four years before, at the age of twenty-one, with five hundred dollars borrowed from a relative. During those four years, his business provided him with a **meager** living, and he worked hard on his films, struggling to pay off the debt.

His cartoons were about a character called Oswald, the Lucky Rabbit. A film distributor in New York had been buying his films and renting them to movie houses. The distributor could make a big profit if a film was successful, but Disney was paid a fixed amount for each movie; he got no share of the profits. When the contract with the distributor came to an end, Walt Disney decided to go to New York with his wife, Lilly, to **negotiate** a better deal for himself.

At the meeting, the distributor not only **declined** all of Disney's proposals, but also told the young filmmaker that he would reduce the payments he was making for each cartoon. He knew very well that Disney had no money to pay lawyers to fight him in the courts. Even worse, the distributor boasted that he had secretly hired Disney's own artists to do the drawings for future Oswald movies. Disney was bitter that the distributor had **betrayed** him, but there was nothing he could do about it. He **vowed** never to sell another of his movies to anyone. He would rent them to distributors, but in the future he would **retain** ownership.

Walt Disney was in a **somber** mood when he and Lilly boarded the train for Los Angeles. During the long journey across the country, he decided to create a new character to take the place of Oswald. After making a few marks on paper, he showed Lilly a sketch of a mouse. Immediately she noticed the **likeness** between her husband and the creature he had drawn; both had a look of harmless **mischief**. She was **convinced** that audiences would love the little mouse with the happy face, but she was dismayed when her husband told her he planned to name it Mortimer. That just didn't sound right to her. "What about Mickey?" she suggested. "Mickey Mouse."

As soon as he arrived in Los Angeles, Walt Disney went to work on the first Mickey Mouse cartoons. He had completed two and was working on *Steamboat Willie*, his third, when sound began to be added to movies. Suddenly silent movies were **obsolete**. Disney promptly added a soundtrack to *Steamboat Willie*. The shrill voice of Mickey was supplied by Walt Disney himself.

When the movie opened in New York in September 1928, it was a **sensation**. Audiences roared with laughter at Mickey's **hilarious** adventures, and **subsequent** movies starring the lovable little mouse were equally successful at the box office. In just three years Walt Disney's company was worth hundreds of thousands of dollars and Mickey Mouse was famous.

animated
betray
convince
decline
hilarious
likeness
meager
mischief
negotiate
obsolete
retain
sensation
somber
subsequent
vow

Answer each of the following questions in the form of a sentence. If a question does not contain a vocabulary word from this lesson's word list, use one in your answer. Use each word only once. Questions and answers will then contain all fifteen words (or forms of the words).

1. How would you describe Walt Disney's income in 1927?

2. What work did Walt Disney do?

3. What is the meaning of **sensation** as it is used in the passage?

4. Why did Disney want to meet with the distributor?

5. Why didn't Disney get a lawyer and sue the New York distributor?

6. How did the distributor respond to Disney's proposals for a new contract?

7. What is the meaning of **betrayed** as it is used in the passage?

8. What **mischief** did the distributor boast of to Disney?

9. What is the meaning of **somber** as it is used in the passage?

10. What lesson did Disney learn from his experience with the distributor?

11. What did Lilly notice about the little mouse Walt Disney had drawn?

_____

12. Why do you think silent movies became **obsolete**?

_____

13. What did Lilly do when her husband suggested the name of Mortimer Mouse?

_____

14. How many Disney movies, after *Steamboat Willie*, had sound?

_____

15. Why did audiences enjoy *Steamboat Willie*?

_____

 FUN & FASCINATING FACTS

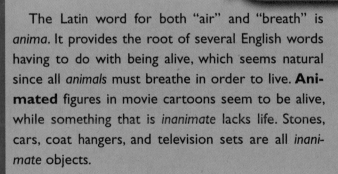

The Latin word for both "air" and "breath" is *anima*. It provides the root of several English words having to do with being alive, which seems natural since all *animals* must breathe in order to live. **Animated** figures in movie cartoons seem to be alive, while something that is *inanimate* lacks life. Stones, cars, coat hangers, and television sets are all *inanimate* objects.

~~~~~~~~~~~~~~~~~~~~~~~~~~~~~~~~

The adjective **somber** comes from the Latin word for "shade," which is *umbra*. Other words formed from this root include *umbrella,* which not only keeps off the rain but provides shade in bright sunlight, and *sombrero,* a Spanish or Mexican broad-brimmed hat worn to provide shade for the face.

Word List
Study the definitions of the words below; then do the exercises for the lesson.

dormant
dôr´ mənt

adj. 1. In a sleeplike state.
Ground hogs remain **dormant** through the winter.
2. Not active, but able to become active.
Japan's Mount Fuji is a **dormant** volcano.

elegant
el´ ə gənt

adj. Graceful or refined in appearance or behavior.
The tiny curved numbers and the slender hands made the old silver watch an **elegant** timepiece.

erupt
ē rupt´

v. To burst forth violently.
The queen **erupted** in anger when told she must abdicate.
eruption *n.* A violent bursting forth.
The **eruption** of Mount Saint Helens in 1980 caused immense damage.

excavate
eks´ kə vāt

v. 1. To dig out.
The backhoe will **excavate** this spot near the pine tree to create the basement of our new house.
2. To uncover by digging.
Heinrich Schliemann began to **excavate** the ancient city of Troy in 1871.
excavation *n.* The place formed by digging or the process of digging out.
The **excavation** of Cahuachi, Peru, uncovered many pieces of pottery from the ancient Nazca culture.

expel
ek spel´

v. 1. To eject; to release, as from a container.
Electric cars help keep the air clean because they don't **expel** poisonous gases.
2. To force to leave.
The school reserves the right to **expel** students for serious offenses.

fume
fyo͞om

n. (usually plural) A disagreeable smoke or gas.
Fumes from passing trucks and buses have damaged the oak trees.
v. To feel or show anger or resentment.
My father **fumed** when he discovered that I had left my bicycle out in the rain all night.

molten
mōlt´ n

adj. Made liquid by heat; melted.
At Colonial Williamsburg, we watched women make tapers by pouring **molten** wax into thin molds.

painstaking
pānz´ tāk iŋ

adj. Showing or taking great care or effort.
After a **painstaking** search of the house, we found our missing car keys.

perish
per´ ish

v. To die; to be killed or destroyed.
Approximately ten million people **perished** in World War I.

population päp yoo lā´ shən	*n.* 1. The total number of people in a certain place. The **population** of the town declined by almost a quarter over the past decade. 2. The total number of plants or animals in a certain area. The elm tree **population** decreased greatly after the 1930s because of Dutch elm disease. **populate** *v.* To fill with people. The English began to **populate** Australia at the end of the eighteenth century.
prelude prel´ yood	*n.* 1. Something that comes before or introduces the main part. The October frost was a **prelude** to a harsh winter. 2. A short musical piece played as an introduction. Suzanne played a piano **prelude** for the spring recital.
scald skôld	*v.* To burn with hot liquid or steam. Boiling water from the overturned saucepan **scalded** the child's leg. **scalding** *adj.* Very hot. The bath water was **scalding**, so I added some cold water.
stupendous stoo pen´ dəs	*adj.* Amazing because it is very great or very large. It took a **stupendous** effort to return the beached whales to the water.
suffocate suf´ ə kāt	*v.* To kill or die by stopping access to air. The trapped miners **suffocated** when their air supply was cut off. **suffocation** *n.* The act or process of suffocating. Keep plastic bags away from young children to avoid any chance of **suffocation**.
tremor trem´ ər	*n.* 1. A shaking movement. **Tremors** following the 1994 Los Angeles earthquake continued for several weeks. 2. A nervous or excited feeling. When I heard the front door creak open, a **tremor** of fear ran through me.

dormant
elegant
erupt
excavate
expel
fume
molten
painstaking
perish
population
prelude
scald
stupendous
suffocate
tremor

19A Finding Meanings

Choose two phrases to form a sentence that correctly uses a word from Word List 19. Write each sentence in the space provided.

1. (a) forbid people to go into it.
   (b) fill it with people.
   (c) To populate an area is to
   (d) To excavate an area is to

2. (a) To perish
   (b) is to tire easily.
   (c) To fume
   (d) is to die.

3. (a) break up into smaller parts.
   (b) burst out violently.
   (c) To suffocate is to
   (d) To erupt is to

4. (a) An excavated building is one   (c) that is beautifully designed.
     (b) An elegant building is one   (d) that has been completely rebuilt.

5. (a) that is amazingly large.   (c) A stupendous job is one
     (b) A painstaking job is one   (d) that is very boring.

6. (a) To scald is   (c) to burn with a hot liquid.
     (b) To expel is   (d) to taunt.

7. (a) To be painstaking is to   (c) take very great care.
     (b) be careless of others' feelings.   (d) To be dormant is to

8. (a) be prevented from getting air.   (c) To erupt is to
     (b) be permited to enter.   (d) To suffocate is to

9. (a) Something that is molten is   (c) made liquid by heat.
     (b) easily damaged.   (d) Something that is dormant is

10. (a) Fumes are   (c) harmful gases.
      (b) Tremors are   (d) burns caused by hot liquids.

19B Just the Right Word

Improve each of the following sentences by crossing out the bold phrase and replacing it with a word (or a form of the word) from Word List 19.

1. **His being unable to breathe** was the cause of his death.

2. When the pipe broke, there was a sudden **bursting out** of steam.

3. The **total number of people living in the city** of New York is around seven million.

4. Some of the passengers began to **feel very angry** when told the train would be an hour late.

5. Chopin transformed the **short musical piece played as an introduction** into a form that is complete in itself.

6. The maple trees that line the driveway are **in an inactive state with no signs of life** during the winter.

7. Parkinson's disease causes **rapid back and forth shaking movements** in the hands.

8. The Martian volcano known as Olympus Mons is **amazing because of its great size**.

9. The **process of digging a hole in the ground** revealed the remains of an ancient Chinese temple.

10. The school suspended the minor offenders, but those guilty of major offenses were **forced to leave for good**.

19C Applying Meanings

Circle the letter of each correct answer to the questions below. A question may have more than one correct answer.

1. Which of the following could be **excavated**?
   (a) a hole
   (b) a secret
   (c) soil
   (d) a buried city

2. Which of the following can be **dormant**?
   (a) a volcano
   (b) a rock
   (c) a tree
   (d) an animal

3. Which of the following can **scald** someone?
   (a) a hot beverage
   (b) a hot iron
   (c) a hot temper
   (d) a hot day

4. Which of the following could be **elegant**?
   (a) an aroma
   (b) a restaurant
   (c) a meal
   (d) a dress

5. Which of the following can **perish**?
   (a) people
   (b) time
   (c) hope
   (d) freedom

6. Which of the following can cause **tremors**?
   (a) a sickness
   (b) an earthquake
   (c) excitement
   (d) fear

dormant
elegant
erupt
excavate
expel
fume
molten
painstaking
perish
population
prelude
scald
stupendous
suffocate
tremor

7. Which of the following can **erupt**?

    (a) an excited crowd   (c) an active volcano

    (b) a riot   (d) an angry character

8. Which of the following can give off **fumes**?

    (a) a faulty oil furnace   (c) an angry person

    (b) a car's exhaust   (d) a lighted oil lamp

19D Word Study

The prefix *ex-* means "out" (an exit is a way out).

Supply the missing word in each sentence below. Choose each word from the list given at the end of the exercise.

1. To _____ cream from milk is to take the cream out.

2. To _____ is to cry out for joy.

3. To become _____ is to die out completely.

4. To _____ is to try something out to see if it works.

5. To _____ something is to send it out of the country.

6. To _____ is to spread out.

7. To _____ someone is to force that person out.

8. To _____ something is to dig it out of the ground.

9. To _____ someone is to wear out that person's patience.

10. To _____ is to breathe out.

exult	excavate	expel	extract	extinct
export	expand	experiment	exasperate	exhale

Read the passage below; then complete the exercise that follows.

The Lost City

Two thousand years ago, Pompeii was a prosperous town with a **population** of perhaps twenty thousand people. It was a busy port located on the Sarnus River, near the Bay of Naples, about a hundred and thirty miles south of Rome. Rich landowners and retired Roman citizens built **elegant** homes in the town and paid for its fine public buildings and temples. The town nestled in the shadow of four-thousand-foot high Mount Vesuvius, and the local farmers cultivated grapes in the mountainside's fertile soil as they had done for centuries.

In A.D. 62, the town was shaken by **tremors** from an earthquake; for the next seventeen years, the people worked to repair the damage. They were not then aware of the danger they were in, but if they had known what we know today, that earthquake would have been a warning to them. **Stupendous** forces were slowly building deep beneath the surface; the earthquake was merely the **prelude** to a far worse disaster.

Vesuvius is a volcano, but it had been **dormant** for eight hundred years. There had been no activity during this time because a thick layer of **molten** rock, called lava, had hardened to form a plug, sealing off the mouth of the volcano like a cork in a bottle. Over the centuries, pressure deep below the earth's surface had been slowly building up inside the volcano. On August 24, A.D. 79, it became so great that the plug of lava was suddenly **expelled** in a tremendous explosion.

So violent was the explosion that the top of the mountain was blown off. Cracks appeared in the earth, and water, heated to boiling by fires beneath the earth's crust, thrust its way to the surface. People and animals were **scalded** as they tried to flee. Smoke, poisonous **fumes**, and ash from the volcano filled the air, **suffocating** many people in their homes. Buildings were crushed by huge rocks hurled from the volcano. Then came a series of avalanches that buried the town, together with everything in it, in twenty feet of stones, cinders, and volcanic ash.

A vivid description of the **eruption** of Vesuvius was given by Pliny the Younger, who later became a famous Roman statesman. He was eighteen years old at the time, and he watched the disaster from twenty miles away on the other side of the bay. His uncle sailed to Pompeii to save the lives of some friends, but died during the attempt. Pliny the Younger described the tragic events of that day in letters he wrote many years later.

For centuries Pompeii lay buried and forgotten. It was not until 1763 that the **excavation** of the ruins first began. **Painstaking** digging revealed streets and buildings filled with the objects of everyday life. Also uncovered were the bodies of the more than two thousand people who **perished** on that terrible day nearly two thousand years ago when the sleeping volcano suddenly woke up.

dormant
elegant
erupt
excavate
expel
fume
molten
painstaking
perish
population
prelude
scald
stupendous
suffocate
tremor

Answer each of the following questions in the form of a sentence. If a question does not contain a vocabulary word from this lesson's word list, use one in your answer. Use each word only once. Questions and answers will then contain all fifteen words (or forms of the words).

1. What did the **excavations** at Pompeii reveal?

2. Why were the citizens of Pompeii unconcerned about Mount Vesuvius?

3. What is the meaning of **prelude** as it is used in the passage?

4. What evidence is there that some of Pompeii's people were wealthy?

5. What is the meaning of **tremors** as it is used in the passage?

6. What happened when the pressure inside the volcano became too great?

7. Why did the explosion of Vesuvius have such **stupendous** force?

8. What materials were thrust from the volcano when it exploded?

9. What is the meaning of **expelled** as it is used in the passage?

10. Why do you think uncovering Pompeii was such **painstaking** work?

11. Why did the underground water from Vesuvius cause deaths and injuries?

12. Why was the air at Pompeii dangerous to breathe?

13. What happened to Pliny the Younger's uncle?

14. How large was Pompeii?

15. What were the three major causes of death at Pompeii?

FUN & FASCINATING FACTS

The dormouse is a European animal resembling a small squirrel. It hibernates in winter. This sleeplike state is what gives it its name: the Latin for "sleep" is *dormire*. The first part of this word combines with *mouse* to form *dormouse*. Other English words formed from this Latin word are **dormant** and *dormitory*, a place where people sleep.

The noun and adjective *perishable* are formed from the verb **perish**. *Perishable* foods spoil quickly, and *perishables* are any foods, such as tomatoes and lettuce, that spoil quickly.

What do *premature* (Word List 3), *previous* (Word List 5), *predict* (Word List 15), and **prelude** all have in common? All four are formed from the Latin prefix *pre-*, which means "before." And notice where a *prefix* is found. It comes *before* the rest of the word.

Lesson 20

Word List
Study the definitions of the words below; then do the exercises for the lesson.

ample
am´ pəl

adj. 1. Plenty; more than enough.
One large turkey will provide **ample** food for eight people.
2. Large in size.
A heavy gold watch chain hung across his **ample** stomach.

burden
bʉrd´ n

n. 1. Something that is carried, especially a heavy load.
Carrying his frail son on his shoulder was never a **burden**, Bob Cratchit explained.
2. Anything that is hard to bear.
The **burden** of caring for four sick children was too much for the babysitter.
v. To add to what one has to bear.
Don't **burden** your grandparents with this problem.

compassion
kəm pash´ ən

n. A feeling of sharing the suffering of others and of wanting to help; sympathy; pity.
Shazia's **compassion** for the homeless led to her working each weekend at the soup kitchen.
compassionate *adj.* The state of showing compassion.
The doctor's **compassionate** manner made her loved by all of her patients.

comply
kəm plī´

v. To act in agreement with a rule or another's wishes.
Unless you **comply** with the requirement to wear shoes, you cannot enter the restaurant.

cumbersome
kum´ bər səm

adj. Awkward and hard to handle; unwieldy.
The crate of oranges was **cumbersome**, but the clerk managed to get it up the stairs.

distress
di stres´

v. To cause pain or sorrow; to trouble or worry.
It **distresses** me that no one offered to help when they saw the accident.
n. Pain, sorrow, or worry.
The **distress** of a divorce is felt especially hard by the children involved.

encounter
en koun´ tər

v. 1. To meet unexpectedly.
The actress **encountered** a crowd of fans in the lobby of her hotel.
2. To be faced with.
As the frightened children ran around the corner, they **encountered** a stone wall.
n. 1. A chance meeting.
Our **encounter** with our neighbors at the party was a pleasant surprise.
2. A battle or fight.
The first major **encounter** of the Civil War occurred at Fort Sumter on April 12, 1861.

exert
eg zʉrt´

v. To put forth effort.
If Jane doesn't **exert** herself more in Spanish class, I'm sure she will not be able to speak the language.
exertion *n.* The act of tiring oneself; a strong effort.
The **exertion** of climbing to the top of the ruins left the explorers feeling weak.

indignant
in dig´ nənt

adj. Angry or resentful about something that seems wrong or unfair.
Bonnie was **indignant** when Miss Slighcarp, her governess, appeared in the most elegant dress Bonnie's mother owned.
indignation *n.* Anger that is caused by something mean or unfair.
My **indignation** was aroused when I was not given a chance to defend myself.

jest
jest

n. A joke or the act of joking.
My remark was made in **jest**; I'm sorry you took me seriously.
v. To joke or say things lightheartedly.
"Surely you **jest**," I said when my aunt suggested throwing out the television set.

mirth
mᴜrth

n. Laughter; joyfulness expressed through laughter.
The sight of the three-year-old wearing her mother's hat and shoes provoked much **mirth** among the family.

moral
môr´ əl

n. A useful lesson about life.
The play's **moral** was "Look before you leap."
adj. 1. Having to do with questions of right and wrong.
The death sentence for murder is a **moral** as well as a legal issue.
2. Based on what is right and proper.
You have a **moral** duty to report a crime if you see it.

outskirts
ᴏut´ skᴜrts

n. The parts far from the center, as of a town.
The plan to build another large shopping mall on the **outskirts** of town was voted down at the meeting.

resume
re zᴏᴏm´

v. 1. To begin again after a pause.
The concert will **resume** after a fifteen-minute break.
2. To occupy again.
After the station stop, the detective **resumed** his seat for the next part of the journey.

ridicule
rid´ i kyᴏᴏl

v. To make fun of; to mock.
People once **ridiculed** the idea that flight by heavier-than-air machines was possible.
n. Words or actions intended to make fun of or mock.
Their **ridicule** of my friend finally provoked me to lose my temper.
ridiculous *adj.* Laughable; deserving of mockery.
It is **ridiculous** to suggest that a bridge could be built across the Atlantic Ocean.

ample
burden
compassion
comply
cumbersome
distress
encounter
exert
indignant
jest
mirth
moral
outskirts
resume
ridicule

20A Finding Meanings

Choose two phrases to form a sentence that correctly uses a word from Word List 20. Write each sentence in the space provided.

1. (a) is crudely made.
   (b) is awkward to handle.

   (c) A ridiculous object is one that
   (d) A cumbersome object is one that

2. (a) Mirth is
   (b) Distress is

   (c) a calm and untroubled state.
   (d) joy expressed by laughter.

3. (a) An indignant reply   (c) is one that expresses pity.
   (b) A compassionate reply   (d) reveals a deep hatred of others.

4. (a) To encounter someone is to (c) To distress someone is to
   (b) make that person suffer.   (d) feel sorry for that person.

5. (a) Outskirts are   (c) useful lessons about life.
   (b) Morals are   (d) customs that are no longer practiced.

6. (a) anger caused by unfairness. (c) Exertion is
   (b) Indignation is   (d) wrongful behavior.

7. (a) Jests are   (c) parts far from the center.
   (b) Outskirts are   (d) things that are hard to bear.

8. (a) a slow, heavy walk.   (c) A burden is
   (b) An encounter is   (d) a chance meeting.

9. (a) continue it after a pause. (c) To resume a speech is to
   (b) To ridicule a speech is to   (d) bring it to a sudden end.

10. (a) A jest is   (c) something that is hard to bear.
    (b) A burden is   (d) a lesson that teaches right and wrong.

20B Just the Right Word

Improve each of the following sentences by crossing out the bold phrase and replacing it with a word (or a form of the word) from Word List 20.

1. Caring for Father after he broke his leg **put a load that was hard to bear on** me.

2. The runners were asked to **go back to** their places after the false start.

3. We were **filled with anger over the unfairness of it** when the library had to cut back its hours.

4. I kept my diary secret to avoid my little brother's **making fun of me**.

5. You must have known that I spoke in **a way that was not intended to be taken seriously**.

6. I have **more than enough** spending money for my vacation.

7. In an emergency, if you are ordered to leave the building, you must **do as you are told**.

8. We were panting after our **efforts that left us tired out**.

9. The **lesson that is the main point** of the story is that "haste makes waste."

10. Following their **meeting in battle**, each side proclaimed victory.

20C Applying Meanings

Circle the letter of each correct answer to the questions below. A question may have more than one correct answer.

1. Which of the following would be **cumbersome**?
   (a) a tennis racket   (c) a broken bicycle
   (b) a heavy suitcase   (d) a photo album

2. Which of the following might be a **burden**?
   (a) a load of firewood   (c) a pardon
   (b) a sack of potatoes   (d) a debt

3. Which of the following can one **resume**?
   (a) a conversation   (c) a journey
   (b) one's seat   (d) a destination

4. Which of the following might cause one to feel **compassion**?
   (a) a strange noise   (c) a disaster
   (b) a homeless person   (d) starving people

5. Which of the following might cause **mirth**?
   (a) a bee sting   (c) a tickling in the ribs
   (b) a hilarious story   (d) a plane's sudden loss of power

ample

burden

compassion

comply

cumbersome

distress

encounter

exert

indignant

jest

mirth

moral

outskirts

resume

ridicule

6. Which of the following might a person **encounter**?
   (a) difficulties   (c) a serious problem
   (b) a school friend   (d) hostility

7. For which of the following must one **exert** oneself?
   (a) watching TV   (c) climbing stairs
   (b) falling asleep   (d) running a marathon

8. Which of the following is the **moral** thing to do?
   (a) to cheat on a test   (c) to choose vanilla over strawberry
   (b) to admit that one lied   (d) to return a lost wallet to its owner

20D Word Study

Look at each group of four words below. If you think two of the words in a group are synonyms, circle those words and write *S* in the space next to the words. If you think two of the words in a group are antonyms, circle those words and write *A* in the space next to the words.

1. dense	primitive	crude	absurd	_____
2. require	dominate	retain	keep	_____
3. animated	sluggish	formal	brittle	_____
4. fascinate	topple	prohibit	overthrow	_____
5. pity	prelude	aroma	compassion	_____
6. mirth	laughter	option	pasture	_____
7. bland	flimsy	sparse	meager	_____
8. visible	drab	elegant	dormant	_____
9. bungle	jest	joke	budge	_____
10. careless	fearful	delicate	painstaking	_____
11. somber	jubilant	accurate	available	_____
12. die	hoist	perish	denounce	_____
13. decline	huddle	accept	celebrate	_____
14. lure	moral	meeting	encounter	_____
15. frivolous	barren	fertile	feeble	_____

Read the passage below; then complete the exercise that follows.

A Tale of Two Donkeys

Aesop was a slave who lived in ancient Greece. Although little is known about his life, readers have enjoyed the fables he told for more than twenty-five centuries. Not only are his stories entertaining, but they also teach us something about human behavior, for a fable is a story with a lesson. The characters in them can be animals who talk and behave like humans, or they can be ordinary people, like those in the story that follows.

A farmer and his daughter were on their way to market to sell a donkey, the farmer riding on the animal's back while the daughter plodded along at his side. After they had gone about a mile, they happened to **encounter** a woman drawing water from a well. She was very **indignant** at the sight of the farmer riding in ease while his daughter had to walk. She told the farmer that he should be ashamed of himself. So, to please her, the father and daughter changed places. When the young woman was sitting comfortably on the donkey, they **resumed** their journey.

Just as they reached the **outskirts** of the town, they met a young man who asked the farmer why he was walking when there was **ample** room for both of them on the donkey. To please the young man, the father climbed onto the donkey behind his daughter and they continued on their way.

A little later they passed by two women standing by the side of the road. When they saw the donkey carrying two grown people, the women were filled with **compassion** for the animal. "Have you any idea of the **distress** you are causing that poor donkey?" the older woman called out to the farmer. "The poor creature is half dead from having to carry such a **burden**." The younger woman loudly remarked that the farmer and his daughter should be carrying the donkey instead of the donkey carrying them. She spoke in **jest**, but the farmer took her seriously and at once set about to **comply** with her suggestion.

First, he tied the donkey's legs to a pole. This took some time, as the donkey had no desire to have its legs tied, but at last the task was accomplished. Such a **cumbersome** load was difficult for the farmer and his daughter to lift. But finally, they managed to hoist the pole onto their shoulders. With the donkey slung upside down between them and struggling to escape, they staggered down the road.

At last, panting from their **exertions**, they reached the market. Their arrival was greeted with considerable **mirth**, so that when the farmer tried to sell the donkey, his attempts were **ridiculed**. For, of course, no one was willing to buy a donkey that had to be carried.

Can you guess the **moral** of this fable? The Hidden Message puzzle in the review section at the end of this lesson will spell it out for you.

ample

burden

compassion

comply

cumbersome

distress

encounter

exert

indignant

jest

mirth

moral

outskirts

resume

ridicule

Answer each of the following questions in the form of a sentence. If a question does not contain a vocabulary word from this lesson's word list, use one in your answer. Use each word only once. Questions and answers will then contain all fifteen words (or forms of the words).

1. How do you think people responded when Aesop told this story?

2. How do you think the ending of the story would have changed if the farmer and his daughter had not **encountered** anyone on the way to town?

3. What reason do you think Aesop had for telling this story?

4. Why might one feel **compassion** for the farmer's daughter?

5. Why do you think the farmer never became **indignant** when people kept telling him what to do?

6. How did the farmer respond to the various suggestions that were made?

7. What is the meaning of **burden** as it is used in the passage?

8. In what way did the farmer misunderstand the young woman who suggested that he and his daughter should carry the donkey?

9. What do you think probably **distressed** the donkey most?

10. Why would it be difficult for two people to carry a donkey?

11. What is the meaning of **resumed** as it is used in the passage?

12. How does the passage make clear that the farmer and his daughter found carrying the donkey hard work?

13. What is the meaning of **ample** as it is used in the passage?

14. Where were the farmer and his daughter when they met the young man?

15. How do you think the farmer and his daughter must have looked when they reached the market?

FUN & FASCINATING FACTS

The Greek word *pathos*, which means "suffering," has passed unchanged into English via Latin. It means "something that moves a person to feel pity." By combining the Latin root with the prefix *con* (also written *com-* or *col-*), which means "with" or "together," we form the word **compassion**. Several other words are formed from this root. *Sympathy* has the same meaning as *compassion*, although the latter term suggests a greater depth of feeling. *Pathetic* means "arousing feelings of pity." (The *pathetic* cries of the injured animal moved us to tears.)

~~~~~~~~~~~~~~~~~~~~~~~~~~~~

The language spoken in France from the ninth to the early sixteenth century is called Old French. The Old French verb *encombrer* meant "to put obstacles in the way of." **Cumbersome** and several other English words have been formed from this Old French verb. To *encumber* someone is to put a heavy load on that person. (Hikers who are *encumbered* with heavy backpacks are glad of a chance to rest.) An *encumbrance* is anything that is awkward, difficult, or heavy. (Heavy boots are an *encumbrance* when running to catch a school bus.)

~~~~~~~~~~~~~~~~~~~~~~~~~~~~

Resume is a noun meaning "a brief outline or summary, especially of a person's education and work experience." It is sometimes written with a stroke, or accent, over each e [résumé]. This is done because it is the French spelling, and *resume* is a French word brought into English. With this meaning, the word is pronounced the French way, *REZ-oo-may*.

Review for Lessons 17–20

Hidden Message In the spaces provided to the right of each sentence, write the vocabulary words from Lessons 17 through 20 that are missing in each of the sentences below. Be sure that the words you choose fit the meaning of each sentence and have the same number of letters as there are spaces. The number following each sentence gives the lesson from which the missing word comes. If the exercise is done correctly, the shaded boxes will spell out the moral of Aesop's fable on page 162.

1. Plants _____ if they are not watered. (17)

2. I warned the child not to get into any _____. (18)

3. _____ meetings went much better than the first one. (18)

4. I will _____ my journey in the morning. (20)

5. The waves are starting to _____ the cliff. (17)

6. It would _____ me to see you hurt in any way. (20)

7. I was filled with _____ for the homeless people. (20)

8. The _____ of China is over one billion. (19)

9. These _____ tools are ten thousand years old. (17)

10. I had an odd _____ as though I were being watched. (18)

11. I made a _____ that I would never smoke. (18)

12. A _____ avalanche almost buried the village. (19)

13. Some plants stay _____ over the winter. (19)

14. I was afraid that the smoke would _____ me. (19)

15. The first crocuses are a _____ to spring. (19)

16. We made a _____ search of the building. (19)

17. Don't _____ yourself if you're feeling tired. (20)

18. I tried not to _____ my true feelings. (18)

19. Will you _____ ownership of the house? (18)

20. Did you _____ any problems with the project? (20)

21. A fan is used to _____ hot air from the kitchen. (19)

22. I must _____ your kind offer. (18)

23. Neglected gardens soon _____ to weeds. (17)

24. The comic's _____ jokes made the crowd roar. (18)

25. Our new house is on the _____ of town. (20)

26. The oak wardrobe was a _____ piece of furniture. (20)

27. The _____ glass glowed a bright cherry red. (19)

28. What will you do with the soil that you _____? (19)

29. The disease causes a _____ in the patient's hands. (19)

30. _____ soil produces good crops. (17)

31. A(n) _____ in the Sahara is a welcome sight. (17)

32. Taking a deep breath will _____ your chest. (17)

33. He began to _____ at the long delay. (19)

34. Will you _____ with my request? (20)

35. We hope to _____ a settlement by tomorrow. (18)

36. You must expect _____ if you dress so oddly. (20)

37. The wedding banquet was in a(n) _____ hotel. (19)

38. When crops fail, the result is often _____. (17)

39. I set down my _____ and rested a while. (20)

40. The long _____ ended with a heavy rainstorm. (17)

41. We have _____ time to make it to the airport. (20)

42. Desert areas are mostly _____ and little grows there. (17)

43. He's liable to _____ in anger without any reason. (19)

44. Blindness did not _____ her until she was 70. (17)

45. They will _____ if they are not rescued soon. (19)

46. I could not live on the _____ wage. (18)

47. This field provides good _____ for the horses. (17)

48. My clown costume caused a lot of _____. (20)

49. Do you see a _____ between my cousin and me? (18)

50. We found _____ from the storm in an old hut. (17)

51. How can I _____ you I am telling the truth? (18)

52. The coming of the railroad made stage coaches _____. (18)

53. The funeral put us all in a _____ mood. (18)

54. I was most _____ when told I had been left out. (20)

55. Please don't _____ about such a serious matter. (20)

Review for Lessons 17–20

Crossword Puzzle Solve the crossword puzzle below by studying the clues and filling in the answer boxes. Clues followed by a number are definitions of vocabulary words in Lessons 17 through 20. The number gives the lesson from which the answer to the clue is taken.

Clues Across

1. Alive or seeming to be alive (18)
4. Dark and gloomy (18)
10. To make or become larger (17)
12. Not able to produce crops (17)
13. A remark made jokingly (20)
14. No longer in use; out-of-date (18)
15. Fruit of the palm tree
16. An area with water in a desert (17)
18. To be angry (19)
23. To go back to an earlier condition (17)
24. To be filled with; to overflow with (17)
25. Good or proper (20)
26. A widespread and longlasting food shortage (17)
27. What noses do
28. Something that comes before the main part (19)

Clues Down

2. Laughter (20)
3. A shaking movement (19)
5. Opposite of "even"
6. Holy book made up of Old and New Testaments
7. To be made up (17)
8. To burst out violently (19)
9. To be disloyal to (18)
11. Grassland where animals can feed (17)
15. Pain, sorrow, or worry (20)
17. To burn with hot liquid (19)
19. Graceful; pleasingly designed (19)
20. To hold onto; to keep (18)
21. Small in amount (18)
22. To wear away bit by bit (17)
23. Opposite of "lower"